MY FORMERLY HOT LIFE

Dispatches from <u>*Just*</u> *the Other Side of Young*

STEPHANIE DOLGOFF

This is a work of nonfiction, however, some of the names
and personal characteristics of the individuals involved
have been changed in order to disguise their identities.
Any resulting resemblance to persons living or dead
is entirely coincidental and unintentional.

Published in the United States by Ballantine Books,
an imprint of The Random House Publishing Group,
a division of Random House, Inc., New York.

BALLANTINE and colophon are registered trademarks
of Random House, Inc.

LIBRARY OF CONGRESS CATALOGING-IN-PUBLICATION DATA
Dolgoff, Stephanie.
My formerly hot life : dispatches from just the other side of youth / Stephanie Dolgoff.
p.   cm.
ISBN 978-0-345-52145-3 (hbk. : alk. paper)
1. Women—Psychology.   2. Middle-aged women—Psychology.   3. Aging—
Psychological aspects.   4. Dolgoff, Stephanie.   I. Title.
HQ1206.D62 2010
305.244'20973090511—dc22   2010015092

Printed in the United States of America
on acid-free paper

www.ballantinebooks.com

2 4 6 8 9 7 5 3 1

FIRST EDITION

Book design by Jo Anne Metsch

CONTENTS

CONTENTS

MY FORMERLY
HOT LIFE

1

Bitch-Slap Birthday

There were certainly signs that something momentous was taking place, but initially, I saw each as an isolated incident:

• Beginning a couple of years ago, salespeople in trendy boutiques, who used to swirl around me like bees over a puddle of orange soda, could no longer be bothered. Evidently they saw me as someone who wouldn't (or plain shouldn't) buy their skinny jeans, spiky heels or strappy little camis that are ideally worn without a bra.

• Friends arriving in New York City asked me—a lifetime Gotham denizen and supposedly glamorous member of the fashion and lifestyle media—which were the cool places to hang out. I couldn't think of one that hadn't been shuttered during the first *90210* era or that wasn't now a Starbucks.

• I began to have to wear makeup, or at least a decent tinted moisturizer, to get that same "I'm not wearing makeup" look that I used to get by, well, not wearing makeup.

• One time, in a Pilates class, the instructor had us lying on our backs, pressing our shoulders into the mat. She then told us to raise our arms straight up, at a 90-degree angle from the floor, and then reach to the sky, lifting just our shoulders. We all did: The bones of my shoulders followed my arms vertically a full four inches toward the ceiling. But the flesh surrounding my shoulder bones remained splooged out on the mat. My skin and the thin layer of adipose tissue that normally traveled with my bones and muscles had clearly decided that Pilates was for losers.

• And the real piercing car alarm of a signal—why this didn't catch my attention I have no idea—came one morning after too much coffee, as I was rocking out in the kitchen to "One Way or Another," a Blondie song seared into my neuropathways since adolescence. I was horrified when I realized it was the sound track to a Swiffer commercial, blaring from the TV in the other room. I found it especially humiliating that there was a Swiffer, at that very moment, sitting in my broom closet. What's more, I had recommended it to friends (!!!). I thought about that: *I feel strongly enough about a cleaning implement to have recommended it to friends.* It didn't seem like that long ago I wasn't spending enough time at my apartment to need to clean.

I began to feel vaguely uneasy, but the reason hadn't yet gelled. Things were going quite well, and my life was more or less exactly as I'd set it up to be: I had lived my lunatic 20s, throwing myself into my career, scaled many magazines' mastheads and then calmed the eff down and gotten married in my mid-30s. My husband and I had wonderful twin little girls, I had a great job, good friends, and we all were healthy and solvent. There was no crisis. And yet . . . something was off.

I just didn't feel like me.

And then, finally, one day just after my 40th birthday, all became blindingly clear.

It was early in the morning and I was on the subway, on my way to work. A sexy stubbly man next to me leaned in and asked me for the time. I braced myself for the pickup attempt I felt sure was to follow. "Eight-forty," I replied tersely, careful not to offer even a hint of encouragement in my tone.

And then . . . nothing. Nada. Bubkes. He may have said, "Thanks." I don't remember. I do remember that he went back to his book. Apparently, the sexy stubbly guy who asked me for the time simply needed to know the time. He wanted information, not to have sex with me. Imagine!

I was shocked. Shocked! And internally embarrassed. Just who the hell did I think I was? Well, I'll tell you who I thought I was! I thought I was who I had always been: a hot chick, damn it! Big hair, big boobs, big personality, a young woman who (not so terribly long ago) had reason to adopt a slightly defensive posture when men asked her superficially innocent questions on public transportation. (In fact, I met the man who is now my husband on the subway.) I was hardly a supermodel, but hey, even if I wasn't a particular person's type, it seemed to me that my general appeal was irrefutable. After a few decades of believing this about myself—and usually being reacted to as if it was so—being an attractive young woman simply became part of what I was and how I navigated the world.

But in that instant, an energy-saver bulb reluctantly flickered on over my head, and I got it. Boy, did I ever get it. I was no longer "all that," perhaps no longer even a little of "that," whatever "that" is. No wonder things didn't feel right! I didn't feel like me anymore because I wasn't me, at least not the me I had always been.

I'm not talking about one guy's opinion, of course. In retrospect, all the indications that my head-turner days were receding in the rearview were there (in addition to the aforementioned, fewer men who drink 40s on apartment stoops made vile sucking noises as I walked by; and I was ma'amed on several occasions when I was not in the Deep South). Together, along with all the other signs that had nothing to do with my looks, it made sense. Over the last few years, while I'd been busy working and having twins and not sleeping and getting peed on and eating and yelling at my husband and maybe not taking such good care of myself—and oh, yes, that pesky passage of time thing—I'd become a perfectly nice-looking 40-year-old working mom doing the best she can. Which is *totally not the same* as a hot chick. That in itself is not a problem. The problem was that my self-definition had yet to catch up with the reality of what the world saw when it looked at me.

Lucky for me, I had my then-four-year-old daughter Vivian, at home to give my self-definition a good frog-march forward. That very same evening, she snuggled close to me on the chair-and-a-half in her bedroom while I brushed her hair after her bath. Abruptly, she turned to me.

"Mommy, what are those?" she asked, her face just millimeters from mine, so close that her eyes were crossing. She was fixated on my nose.

"What are what, honey?"

"Those. Those round things." We'd been over this. That Japanese book, *The Holes in Your Nose,* about nostrils and boogers and which body orifices you might stick your fingers in and which you are firmly discouraged from sticking your fingers in, had long been a favorite in our house. I reminded her that they were my nostrils and that she had them, too.

"No, not those. Those smaller ones. Some of them have little hairs growing from them."

Sigh. Vivian, of course, was referring to my pores, which in the last couple of years had been expanding like crop circles on my face. I'd hoped no one had noticed the little hairs. I can only see them in the 15× magnification mirror I masochistically keep in the bathroom.

I felt that familiar wave of . . . not shame, not humiliation, exactly—you can hardly be ashamed of your pores in front of your child—but of what I'd imagine a toad would feel if he were cognizant of being dissected: laid bare, with the cool, objective, curious eyes of a scientist seeking data. This same scenario had repeated itself many times in the last year with little variability, except regarding which of my previously unremarked-upon flaws was being scrutinized.

So I did what I did the time her sister, Sasha, pointed out—entirely without judgment—that my belly looked like a tushy on the front of my body, or the time she said that there were bumpy blue worms under the skin of my legs: I chuckled wisely and said something mature about how bodies are fascinating and change as they get older and went and got the 15× magnification mirror and showed Vivian her own (invisible to the naked eye) pores. I then explained the function of pores in cooling the body. Vivian was riveted. I was proud of myself for being such a good mommy, for recognizing and acting on one of those "teachable moments" you read about in the parenting magazines.

And then she asked this:

"But why would there be hairs in your pores?"

Yeah, you know, Vivian, I'd like to know the same ★(^&(*$@★&^ thing!!! Maybe it's because there is no God, Vivian. Maybe it's because your mommy did something really, really naughty in a former life. Maybe because the body is just randomly gross for no reason and we're all basically still monkeys and some things are simply better examined from a distance. "I just don't know, sweetheart," I answered. And then I put her to bed, and took the 15× magnification mirror with me to see what I could do with a tweezer.

That pair of entirely un-fun epiphanies indicated that there was a seismic, unacknowledged transition afoot. It felt like a smack upside the head and a relief at the same time. I didn't know what I was turning into, exactly. I didn't act, look or feel what I'd imagine a middle-aged person would look, act or feel like, and I certainly wasn't old. I just knew that I wasn't what I used to be. I had been unsubtly hot, and now, I supposed, I wasn't. I began jokingly calling myself Formerly Hot. At least I had a name (albeit one I made up) for that strange, uneasy, dissonant feeling I was having, and why I was having it.

Formerly Hot. Yes, that felt right, and it made me laugh at myself, which seemed the better alternative to standing in front of the mirror scrutinizing my multiplying crow's-feet. And although I didn't yet grasp the extent of this new state of affairs, I had a feeling that there was much more going on than the blush falling off the rose, and that I couldn't be the only one experiencing something like it. If years of writing and editing stories for women's magazines has taught me anything, it's that if you're going through something, odds are excellent you're not that special—quite often in a good, comforting way.

I began to carry my new self-definition—that of Formerly—tentatively around with me like a just-in-case sweater, and threw it over my shoulders whenever I had that chilly feeling of being an adult "tween"—i.e., too old to be young but too young to be the kind of person who asks about the availability of parking at her destination before agreeing to go. "Formerly" fit nicely, and now that I had a name for it, I found myself tripping over evidence of my transition everywhere I went and in every interaction I had.

It quickly became clear that no longer being hot was merely the most obvious Formerly I was experiencing. I was also Formerly Groovy, Formerly Relevant and Formerly In-the-Know. I noticed that marketers had stopped trying to sell me cutting-edge, exciting sparkly things and tried to get me to take my children on a Disney cruise or consider baking with Splenda. Physically I felt fit and well (if lumpy and misshapen from childbearing), but I had lost enough energy for it to be noticeable; I no longer felt like staying out all night, and the truth was, I really wasn't sure I could party past 2:00 AM these days even if I wanted to. I liked to get out and do things, but I needed a guarantee it was going to be more fun than staying home, or else why bother? I wasn't crotchety, yet I was irked by things that I used to let roll off me, like rude people and having to sleep on a futon. I started a blog about this, formerlyhot.com, and it clearly struck a chord. I and my agemates were formerly a lot of things, a big bunch of Formerlies. It was a veritable groundswell.

Still, the transition to Formerly was, and is, a process, and for quite some time there were moments I'd forget that I was a Formerly entirely, or that any time had passed at all, really, only to be snapped back to reality. One time on the train (again on the train!) I saw Mike, a guy I knew 15 years ago. He was a bandmate of a guy I was dating at the time, and he looked precisely as he did when I'd last seen him, across a nasty basement club on Bleecker Street that no longer exists: thick-framed retro-nerd glasses, the kind that only the least nerdy among us can pull off. He was short but had a swagger, and always seemed to feel that he was more talented than the rest of his band and that no one realized how egregiously they were holding him back. He had his axe strapped to his back, which I took as a good sign—perhaps he'd made it as a working musician, despite the odds.

I snaked across the crowded car to say hi, but the closer I got, the clearer it became: It wasn't Mike, but Mike 2.0, the 2009 model of Mike. It was the guy who is now playing the role of Mike—the short, somewhat arrogant guy in the band who is a friend of someone's boyfriend. He was Mike's replacement. The real Mike, wherever he was, probably no longer looked or acted like Mike. I just knew deep in my gut that the life this guy was living mirrored Mike's in every way, except with a few new bells and whistles, like a nylon backpack contraption to hold his guitar (as opposed to those heavy hard cases they used to carry back in the '90s) and an iPod instead of a Walkman. It was entirely possible that he was wearing Mike's actual motorcycle jacket, as I imagined that Mike's wife donated it to the Salvation Army when he was out of town selling bathroom fixtures or whatever he now does to pay for, say, his daughter's speech therapy. It felt as if the real Mike and the real Stephanie, the ones we used to be, were abducted by aliens and simply replaced by the new Mikes and Stephanies who populate the F train just like we used to.

These kinds of old-friend sightings were truly startling to me, but I suppose I needed to learn, again and again, that after several decades, I was in a different life phase. How bizarre that I was excruciatingly aware of every droopy body part, every pucker, each stray hair and both nasal-labial folds on my own person, but I imagined somehow everyone else was frozen in time, going about their lives as if nothing had changed. I mean, I knew they were not, and yet when I saw these updated versions of people I used to know, and was reminded in such a *Twilight Zone* manner that time marches on, it was unsettling.

Once I realized Mike wasn't Mike, I saw myself through new Mike's eyes: He didn't see the early '90s hot Stephanie coming toward him through the throng, but some harmless lady in yoga pants and sneakers clearly chosen for function over fashion, carrying a child's rolled-up collage with glitter and feathers peeking out of the top. He probably thought, *I must be blocking the subway doors because I can't imagine she'd have anything to say to me.* And it turns out he was right.

The Formerly years hit me when they did because my late 30s were the first chance I had to look up from what I'd been doing and take a breather. I think this is true of many people like me who got on the hamster wheel in high school and kept running until career success or giving birth or something else made us want to (or have to) slow down.

You don't feel as if much has changed in some ways—you still look, dress and socialize as you always did, more or less. But you've slowly been taking on responsibilities and time has been passing and your parents have been getting creaky and you've likely even married and had kids (it's nice that you're a cool parent who appreciates the Killers, but time is still passing). I, for one, took each of these things in stride as I experienced them.

No, it wasn't the milestones I reached that made me feel older. For me it was when I began to not feel like the me I once was. In my case, my self-image as a young, attractive, relevant, in-the-mix woman started to feel wobbly, and probably affected the way I carried myself and behaved. Perhaps because I didn't exude as many young, attractive, relevant, in-the-mix woman vibes (and because I looked like the overwrought working mom with no time to tweeze her eyebrows that I was), people didn't treat me as such, and so I didn't behave as such. It was a self-perpetuating cycle and soon I didn't recognize myself anymore. It made me feel a little cuckoo.

In actuality, most of the physical changes my body and my face had undergone over the last decade or so were gradual and fairly subtle. My ass, for example, which I'd never really paid attention to because, well, it was behind me, was all of a sudden crying out for a bra—I could literally feel it against the backs of my thighs, threatening to merge with them unless I found a way to lift and separate. The people who saw me every day (those would be the people I cared about

most, the only ones who should matter) didn't notice anything different. I looked fine. Each of these little changes (did
I mention my upper arms have recently begun to flap in the
breeze like Grand Opening flags on a car dealership and that
I must daily scan my chin for guy-caliber whiskers or else
grow a beard?) didn't keep me up at night.

But in aggregate, and because they all added up to my
being in a brand-new category of person—that of the not-
young woman—they bothered me. A lot. Was I really so
vain that I cared about what complete strangers thought?

Why, yes, yes I was! Which was yet another blow to my
self-definition: After overcoming an eating disorder when I
was a young adult, I'd been proud to be someone who didn't
dwell inordinately on my looks. I certainly cared, and I liked
to look good, but especially compared to some of the fabulous folks I worked with at various women's magazines, I
didn't get nuts about it. Now it seemed that this was only
because I looked good without *having* to get nuts about it,
not because I was so secure. Ouch.

I quickly learned that being Formerly Hot was not something it was wise to go around complaining about. Talking
about losing your looks, especially when you're the main
person who notices, smacks of a fishing-for-compliments
trip, which was not what I meant to be embarking on. I
knew rationally that I looked fine, and if I didn't, it wasn't
the end of the world. But I wanted to talk about why
it sometimes felt as if it was, and about similar shifts in
identity—the loss of a self-definition, be it the whiz kid, the

wild girl, the people pleaser—I knew from my blog that many people were experiencing. The larger life changes (going off to college, getting married, becoming a parent) had been scrutinized, written about and researched to death in the hallowed halls of this country's most esteemed institutions of higher learning. Not so the more subtle life shifts like the one I was experiencing, which are deceptively difficult to deal with, superficial though some of them may appear to be.

Now that I'm a few years into being a Formerly, I get that the phenomenon is about getting older in general and not as much about any specific aspect of it, such as how your looks change. Everyone gets older at the same rate, of course, but ten minutes seems like a squirmy, intolerable hour to my daughters, who are waiting for me to be done with work so I can pay attention to them; to me, it's a millisecond. Things merely seem more accelerated as you age, and when I think of it that way, the transition to Formerly feels like any other, best dealt with one day at a time.

So I'm a Formerly. What of it? Most of the time, it's kind of terrific over here on the other side of young. There are legions of us, and we're an amazingly cool group of women (and men, by the by, with whom we may have even better relationships than when we were younger). By and large, we know our own minds, are done with caring too much about what other people think of our opinions, and can have a good laugh at our own expense. I love being a Formerly because I'm young enough to have fun, and old enough to know what fun really is, as opposed to tossing my head back in maniacal mirth in order to *seem* like I was having fun because I was young and hot and hence supposed to be having the time of my life. I also know that if I'm not having fun, I can just leave, something that never would have occurred to me when I felt as if I had so much to prove. I'm surrounded with friends who have my back, and the family I've built is the family I've always wanted. I even like the family I was born into now, because everyone's had a chance to get over that whole episode with the Cuisinart, which I maintain wasn't my fault. It's a tremendous time of life, weird limbo transition between young and old notwithstanding.

I'm even coming to terms with leaving the hot girl behind. Except when I'm not. That would be when I'm venting about it on my blog, fantasizing about some magical way to restore my former fabulousness or whining to my husband, who, fortunately for me, is blind or deluded or smart enough to insist I'm as dewy as the day he met me (for this reason alone I will not divorce him). Clearly, I'm still adjusting, but having so many women around me going through the same thing makes it easier, as does, of course, having a bit of perspective. Conveniently, that comes with age.

2

Clothing Crisis

one of my clothes were working for me.

Lest you think this was your standard situation-specific fashion emergency, where you try on two or fifteen outfits before finding one you can see yourself meeting your potential in-laws in, it was not. I'd been experiencing acute paralysis before the closet every morning for months. My preschool daughters would be standing at the door, lunch boxes in hand, their little Care Bears backpacks strapped on, while, standing in only my bra, I'd holler from the bedroom, "Mommy will be just a minute!" I'd wonder if a black leather skirt that once said "downtown rocker chick" now said "Jennifer Leather sofa upholstery."

This was around three years ago, when I was in my late 30s, and looking back, my crisis of fashion was one of the outward manifestations of becoming a Formerly. I was no longer the person I used to be, the person who bought all of these clothes, so it made sense that they didn't feel right on me. It wasn't as if I was going through a stranger's closet—in fact, my jumbled, piled-high, two-tiered closet was like the ten boxes of snapshots I'd been intending to sort for years. Each groovy outfit and item meant something to me when I acquired it, and it might yet mean something to me again. I just didn't know what. I was still figuring out what it meant to be a Formerly, a woman who at that point only knew that she wasn't what she was (young), and was not quite sure what she is or is becoming. How was I supposed to know what to wear?

Clearly, my closet and my self-definition had some work to do, but I was not aware of this on any kind of conscious level. All I knew was I NEEDED TO GO SHOPPING. After that, my brain shut off, which is, I find, when I do my best shopping. I've heard people talk about how they get into "the zone" while making music, during sex or, if they're an athlete, while breaking speed records. That's me while shopping (and, alas, while doing nothing else). More than once I have stopped at J. Crew on the way to yoga, found meditative peace in flipping through the citron and salmon cardigans on their hangers (click, click, click), and bailed on yoga altogether. After a good shopping day, when I collapse atop my bags on my bed, I feel like I'd imagine a hunter would slinging a deer carcass off his shoulder after having dragged it back from the woods on pure adrenaline. The idea of shopping my socks off was exciting enough, for now, anyway, to distract me from the fact that my leather skirt most definitely no longer says "downtown rocker chick," at least when it's being worn by me.

With no particular plan, I raided boutiques large and small. What I learned (and am still learning) in attiring my new Formerly self is a lot about who that woman is. That's what I needed to know, really, more than I needed any single article I came home with.

Except maybe jeans. Oh, I needed jeans, badly. The ones that fit were clearly out of style. The ones that didn't (yeah, no, they hadn't gotten too loose) had a nasty habit of dialing my BlackBerry whenever I carried it in my back pocket. I'd get home after a long day at work and find three messages on my machine from my own ass, recordings of me talking about something that was boring the first time I said it. I hated to part with my pricey "premium denim," whatever that means, but I'd rather have to buy a bigger size than walk around with camel toe. Gross. Sorry.

Shopping for jeans as a Formerly, it turned out, is a special kind of torture. This is not so much because I used to have a better body for jeans, before I had twins and before my metabolism slammed on the breaks at 40 and decided it would tolerate no more Nutella. Of *course* I Formerly Looked Better in Jeans. I have long since factored that in to my new, mature self-image that values such superficial things less (can't you tell?) and adjusted my expectations of what will reflect back at me in the three-way mirror accordingly.

No, what makes jeans-buying so hard these days is that the companies making the jeans and other interesting cloth-ing no longer have names like Lee and Wrangler that by virtue of their ad campaigns conjure fantasies of a sexy cowboy hoisting me up on his horse and galloping away to do untold sexy cowboy things to me in private. Now they have names like "Rich and Skinny" and "Young, Fabulous and Broke." Seriously, the disparity between those labels and my actual life is just too, too vast. I stand a better chance of encountering the cowboy on my way to pick up my children from gymnastics in New York City than being rich and skinny. It makes me feel silly. Worse, it makes me want to shop at Eileen Fisher. After that, you're just a few yoga classes and a hot flash from joining an ashram. I would be OK if that turned out to be my destiny. I'm just not there yet.

I love clothing, but I am not rich or skinny. Nor am I young, fabulous or broke, although I suppose I'd be willing to inch a bit closer to broke if it meant I could buy some more young and fabulous, and maybe a smidge of skinny, while we're at it. (I'm not sure what skinny is measured in; it wouldn't be pounds or inches or hectares or kilojoules or anything.)

The thing about rich, skinny, young, fabulous and broke is that they are all extreme, albeit arguably glamorous, conditions. But I'm less extreme about most everything, a perk of Formerlydom, I'm discovering. I'm not skinny, but neither am I fat. I'm not young, but not old. I'm not fabulous, although I do some things fabulously, and I have enough money so that if my daughters, who are six, need braces so they can be a bit more fabulous when they get older, it's not a huge hardship. Life is no longer one long music video, complete with the dramatic lighting and the outfit to go with it. When I did feel that way, for a few intense, traumatic periods in my 20s, it was electric, to be sure. But it was also debilitating. Nowadays, I'm happy, self-confident and don't take myself too seriously.

I still take myself seriously enough, however, to refuse to buy jeans from the Misses department, and I'm not sure I would laugh if I saw my jeans parodied in a *Saturday Night Live* sketch. If some smart designer wants to make some real bucks off those of us who are willing to tap into the kids' future orthodontia fund for denim that appeals to the Formerly condition, I have some suggestions for brand names. Maybe Formerly Hot is not an image most people would race to identify with, but it's a label I, for one, would be proud to slap on my ass. Others include:

Solvent and Still Viable

Good Credit Score Jeans

Holding Up Pretty Good Jeans

Call Me "Ma'am" at Your Own Risk Jeans

Can Hold a Conversation Jeans

Nothing to Prove Jeans

I've Forgotten More Than You'll Ever Know Jeans

So Over It Jeans

You Wouldn't Believe What I've Been Through Jeans

Yes, They Make Jeans This Big Jeans

You Just Wait Jeans

Talk to Me When You're 30 Jeans

Love that Lycra Jeans

Been There, Did That (Twice) Jeans
Card Me, I Dare You Jeans
Thinking of Giving Up Sugar Jeans
May Need Some Help Getting Pregnant Jeans
Forgiven and Forgotten Jeans
I Need to Rest in the Stairwell Jeans
I Think, Therefore I'm a Formerly Jeans

The point (which I will probably need to learn and re-learn a few more times before it sticks) is that the clothes I wear as a Formerly need to work for and reflect my life as it is, not some weird coked-up version of Mary Kate and Ashley's fabulous life that probably isn't that much fun even for them, poor little urchins with their soulless, hungry eyes.

Still, I occasionally forget this and go so far as to try on backless tops, pencil-leg pants and bras that are cuter than they are supportive. For obvious reasons, I don't buy them anymore. While they still have a place in my imagination, they no longer have a place in my closet.

3

Kept Women

The other night, I met up with two girlfriends, both of them young enough to remember what it was like to go out drinking and enjoy it, but old enough to realize that even one night of moderate revelry these days means they'll pay in ways unfathomable to their younger selves.

Setting up a date with friends used to mean a couple of 30-second phone calls or maybe a group email. Now it involves a series of high-level negotiations, painful compromises, expenditure of precious marital capital and backroom dealings that rival what it takes to pass health-care reform.

Below is more or less the process I went through to overcome the combination of exhaustion, inertia, ever-present responsibilities, spousal scheduling complications and random pediatric dental emergencies to deliver my Formerly butt onto that bar stool next to my friends:

Step 1. Someone, struck by a wave of optimism mixed with nostalgia, blithely suggests we "all meet for a drink one night." Hey, great idea, looking forward, blah de blah. Let's pretend we're unencumbered and free to dispose of our leisure time as we wish! Whee! See you then!

Step 2. She initiates a volley of emails between invited parties—there are maybe seven women that it would be so great to see—in order to come up with a date upon which we can agree. Due to all of our numerous obligations, this date is often several months hence.

Step 3. Two weeks before said date, a second round of email badminton begins between friends and friends' spouses about whether said night is, in fact, OK. Some have treated this date as tentative, preparing themselves emotionally for the likelihood that someone else's needs (their boss's, their kids', their partner's) will trump theirs and prevent them from having ONE GODDAMNED GLASS OF WINE with their friends once in a friggin' blue moon! Bitter? Oh, no. Just really could use that drink.

The email back-and-forth is repeated until a *truly* agreed-upon date is arrived at and everyone is cc'd, followed by phone calls to childcare providers. One if not two or three invitees will drop out. In our case, three women remain: Julie and Kristin and I. There are six children under six and a guinea pig between us.

Step 4. The day before the date, research begins in earnest as to where to go. None of us has been out with any regularity in years so it is unclear which bars/clubs/lounges are still operational, and if people our age ever go there. Slightly younger friends are consulted, half-remembered club names are Googled, nightlife reviews are dug out of the bathroom reading pile. It's a project.

You'd think anyplace where they serve alcohol would be fine, but actually the opposite is true. God forbid we should go out once every six months and wind up someplace that sucks! With the scarcity of free time that coincides with available babysitting, you want to make sure that every social outing is a slam-dunk. No pressure.

Step 5. We arrive at seven, congratulate ourselves on our choice of venue, wonder why it's so empty (Hint: It's seven!) and spend way too much time deciding on our drinks. Each cocktail has to count for, like, five, since we can't tolerate as much as we used to. I order something with the word "sunrise" in the name. It sounds like it might be pink and symbolic of rebirth. Kristin has forgotten to bring her little key chain flashlight and so can't read the drinks menu in the dim lighting. (Key chain flashlight = OK with her. Drugstore reading glasses = So not OK.) She laughs it off and orders her regular, rum and ginger ale. Julie holds the menu at arm's length in one hand, a votive candle near the words in the other. She orders something with an ingredient no one has heard of, as if this will be her only chance to try it. It may well be. Three cocktail trends will have come and gone by her next furlough and she knows it.

Step 6. By 8:30 we're woozy, talking about our children, quoting unwittingly deep things they've said recently (" 'Mommy, why don't the people with more money just share it with the people who have less?' When you really think about it, why *don't* they?"). It gets a bit maudlin.

Step 7. By 9:30, my left eye is twitching from fatigue, several conversational threads have begun with "I love my husband, but . . ." and we're starting to think about how early we have to wake up the next day. Normal people are just trickling in. We're out the door by 9:45, and the next day I feel as I remember feeling the one time I did Jell-O shots at a room-to-room in college. I had but two drinks. We are each down $65 (we ate something, too) but take comfort in the fact that we rarely go out, so hey, big deal, right? We deserve a little fun.

And it *was* fun, just not as much fun as it used to be when my body didn't shut down so early. These days I am awoken at 6:30 by children asking where I hid the baking soda and vinegar because they want to make a volcano like the science dude on TV—on the rug. Plus the people-watching, guy-scoping aspect of the bar scene is pretty well moot when you go out with your married, Formerly girlfriends who you don't see often enough. I want to talk to them, not some random dude who's 15 years younger, even on the off chance that he's got a thing for women who look tired even after they've slept. If I'm going to have a good bonding session with my friends, I'd rather be caffeinated, not sleepy.

Still, the next time someone suggests drinks, I'll most certainly drag my creaky, rotting carcass out to a bar and do it all again. And I'll call it fun, even though it feels like fun's much older half sister from Dad's failed first marriage. Because there is a certain value to swishing into a bar, kid-, husband- and/or boyfriend-free, ordering something with a goofy name and remembering what it's like to have to yell over loud music to be heard. If nothing else, it's lovely to come home, hoarse and tired, and be happy to be there.

And I got to see my girls.

The thing about friendships when you reach your late 30s and early 40s is that even though you have much less time for them, the quality is so, so much better than when you were in your 20s. Fortunately, just as some über-potent medications come in pills the size of a caraway seed, a small dose of friend time has the intended effect. Plus, these friendships are so much easier. With few exceptions, we all seem to have fairly low expectations of one another ("Please—you remembered my birthday *month*! No, no, no, I love you, toooooo!!!") and an understanding of what it takes to meet even those low expectations, given the madness of our Formerly lives. Perhaps that's why when those expectations are unexpectedly surpassed—which they are all the time, in ways small and enormous—my Formerly friendships seem like even more of a gift.

When my girls were in preschool and I was working full-time, maybe three years ago, I had a problem with my brain. The problem was that it had desiccated into a tiny little porous pumice stone rattling around in my skull, no doubt from all the stress chemicals that it had been marinating in since I had the twins. So one day, the teacher sent a note home asking us to send in white tees for the kids to tie-dye, and, what with my pumice stone for a brain, I had no recollection that I had children, let alone that it was tie-dye day. I was digging around in my purse for a dirty tissue or something the girls could tie-dye, when Ronni, a woman I'd recently become friendly with whose daughter was in my girls' class, showed up with a pack of three white T-shirts. She bought the three-pack even though she has but one child because she thought "maybe" I'd forget.

The gratitude I felt at that moment could not have been greater had she given me a chunk of her liver. I almost cried. Seriously. Since then, I've been doing things like that—carrying two Shout Wipes instead of one, calling a friend when I pass a sale in a store I know she likes. I've missed more than my share of showers and birthday dinners—but if you need a Shout Wipe, I'm your gal.

Formerly friendships also have the advantage of being all but drama-free. By now we've been rocked by bona fide, life-wrecking drama and have lost any taste for the manufactured kind that a deep breath, a shred of common sense and a drop of self-reflection could have averted. Gone are the days of friends sleeping with barely dumped exes, strategic non-invitations to events, allegiances forged and jockeying for position or any vestige of junior-high silliness that remained when we were in our early 20s. There is no hierarchy, at least not that I've noticed.

Back in junior high, which was the height, or rather the nadir, of awful female friend pettiness, when you walked into the cafeteria, everyone was already seated in her little clique. As you approached each cluster with your lunch tray, you could feel the vibes emanating—hostile, neutral or mildly welcoming—and from there you decided where to sit. Above all else, a dork was someone who couldn't read the vibes, and plunked herself down where she wasn't wanted, thus opening herself up to possible scorn.

Now, either there are no such vibes, or I've become that dork and have lost the ability to read the sit-here-at-your-own-peril signals. Social hierarchies might be one of the things, like what guys are "really" thinking about you in bed, that Formerlies have become blissfully oblivious to. Either way, it's awesome! If I've been scorned by any of my figurative seating choices lately, I haven't noticed. That seems to be how it is for most of us: We've all been rejected enough times and done enough rejecting for it to cease being interesting. What's more, we know the value of what we're bringing to the table—ourselves!—and would rather enjoy eating alone, if that's what it comes to. But it rarely does.

When I was in my early 20s, I had a close friend who I adored—she was hilarious, loyal, whip-smart and felt likewise about me. We were in the same circle, lived blocks apart, both worked like mad and dated tons. When we weren't barhopping together, we spent much of our free time watching *Party of Five* and shopping and dissecting our many relationships and friendships.

But we had major Issues, the it-really-hurts-me-when-you-[   ] kind of issues that as a Formerly one only has with people we're explicitly committed to. We had sit-down talks about our feelings and cold wars and reached détentes and then fell out again—it was all terribly intense and upsetting and there was much venting to other friends, which only amplified it. She and I constantly felt betrayed and let down by each other. We were like Lauren and Heidi on *The Hills,* except we weren't blond, or morons, or on television. Or rich, with our own clothing lines. OK, we weren't anything like Lauren and Heidi on *The Hills,* except insofar as we were very dramatic. Eventually, we threw up a Berlin Wall and avoided each other.

[An aside here: Can I tell you how wonderful it is to be able to make a Berlin Wall reference and know that every person reading this will have some sentient-being recollection of the Berlin Wall? Formerlies are so great to write for.]

I cannot imagine a friend now, as a Formerly, with whom I could have an unpleasant breakup; things just aren't that combustible. I also can't foresee any come-to-Jesus talks.

First off, few of us are able to finish a sentence without someone needing a cheese stick or a trip to the potty. But more important, it feels as if most Formerlies have reached a tacit agreement that we will not ask any more of one another emotionally than the other can realistically provide. The disappointments are minor, no one gets off on pushing anyone else's buttons (on new friends, we don't even take the time to learn where they are!) and we cut one another as much slack as we know we'll need sometime in the near future, given how complicated everyone's lives are. "I don't expect all things from any one of my friends," says my friend Julie. "I can take what people have to offer, and I don't have to be friends with everybody."

That sounds very free-form, which I suppose Formerly friendships are. And yet, my friendships are closer and more consistently satisfying, even if some are transacted largely over the phone or on Facebook because folks moved to other states for careers and love and the desire to snowboard all the time (something I can't say I relate to, but hey). "I would say that the major trend is from quantity to quality," says my friend Jennifer, who also used to have some very intense and sometimes troublesome relationships. Jennifer undertook two big friend-weeding projects when she approached 30 and again when she approached 40, in which she inventoried which friends she felt had her best interests at heart, which she felt most comfortable around and which brought out her good, as opposed to her not-so-hot, habits. Then she let the others recede. "It's like cleaning out your

clothes. It makes the better friendships seem more sparkly."
My weeding-out process, like most Formerlies', was entirely
passive, though probably just as thorough.

One of my sparklier "new" friendships is actually with
Harlene, the woman on the other side of that Berlin Wall,
which came down at some point when neither of us were
paying attention. We ran into each other at a wedding a
couple of years ago, and both immediately missed what we'd
loved about each other. The rest of it? Maybe it has gone
wherever my perky boobs, voluminous hair and dewy, unlined face have gone. I'm positive all that negative silliness
will never be seen or heard from again. Either Harlene and I
are too busy pushing our husbands' buttons to push each
other's, or we simply no longer feel the need. Besides, our
husbands click, which, if you're a married Formerly, you
know is almost as good as having a friend with a giant, un-
derused beach house or who's a doctor and doesn't mind if
you email her pictures of stupid skin tags you're convinced
are cancer.

The bummer part, of course, is that just when we're self-
sufficient, emotionally generous and secure enough to have
these incredible friendships, who has time? Familied Formerlies have all these other people—some of them wholly
irrational, Goldfish-scarfing, tantrum-throwing, hokey-
pokey-dancing little people—to answer to. Never mind that
we adore these families, are committed to them and wanted
desperately to expand them (in my case paying thousands
for doctors to extract my eggs and mix them with Paul's

sperm to make embryos and then inject them back in me—desperate, right?). They still make it pretty tough to have any other sustained relationship outside of them.

One solution, of course, is to try to make friend-families, entire families with which your family can hang out. Friend-families mean you don't need to feel guilty about taking time away from your family to see your friends. They're tricky business, because there are so many variables, but there was a point, when my twins were toddlers, that I was so desperate for adult company that wasn't my husband (even given my extensive participation, I was mad at him for knocking me up) that I actively sought such families out. Things only clicked with one or two of them. With most of the others, there were either no sparks, extenuating circumstances (perfectly nice parents can breed biters! Who knew?) or the husbands found each other to be big loser dickheads with bad politics. A few of my attempts were outright disasters.

One time, I agitated for a weekend at a friend's house in New Hampshire. I'd known the female half of the couple for 15 years (I'll call her Debbie), and loved her. I knew her husband less well, but he seemed like a good guy to me. They had a swing set and a climbing structure so even if the kids didn't groove they could dangle from things. Fine. But our husbands were like oppositely charged ions, and it was clear both had been "encouraged" a bit too forcibly. First off, Debbie's husband was a Yankees fan. Mine is a lifelong Mets man. Big whoop, right? I now know that wars have been fought over less. And to make matters more uncomfortable, her husband had followed the Dead, smoked pot and wore tie-dyes. Mine follows politics, is more of an endorphin-high kind of guy and basically thought her husband was full of shit. They might have found common ground shooting hoops, had hers not gotten stoned and sulked and read the paper all weekend, and had mine looked up from his Black-Berry for more than 11 seconds. Debbie got to acting overly cheery and accommodating to make up for her husband, and I couldn't penetrate her wall of optimism that this was going to be "such a *fun* weekend!" despite ample evidence that it was not.

In the end, only the kids had an OK time, and protested our leaving as early as we politely could the day after we arrived. On the phone that night, the husbands separated and the equilibrium restored to our friendship, Debbie and I laughed about how stupid it is that we feel responsible for everyone's enjoyment, as if our husbands were not grown men. We resolved to see each other alone next time, or maybe with the kids, and I filed the experience under Live And Learn: You can't just plunk two families down in a sandbox together like toddlers and assume they'll happily make mud pies.

My Formerly friend Kathleen, who has a daughter, echoes the sentiments of many Formerlies when she says that kids are the beginning of the end of your social life. While it's true that being beholden to someone whose bedtime is 7:00 PM can put a real damper on your party schedule,

I can't really blame the wee ones for this (and believe me, I blame them for a lot of things, not least of all for making me see the Hannah Montana movie, which I wound up not hating, which I found hateful in myself, which is their fault, too). In fact, some of my better friends now are newer, parent friends, and I have my kids to thank for them.

I've come to believe that it's the route most of us take to having kids—coupling up—that can make or break friendships as a Formerly. When I first got together with Paul, I was not yet a Formerly, I had no kids and lots of time to hang out, but I remember some of my single friends not being as available when I was free. There was no acrimony, just a longer and longer period between coffee dates. Part of me thought that they assumed they were second choice after Paul and resented that, or maybe they found me boring, now that I didn't have wild anecdotes about guys who had 37 guitars and a futon but no toilet in their apartment.

And perhaps there *was* a mosquito netting of boringness that descended upon me once I stopped being able to contribute such tales, but I also think my friends were respectfully backing away now that I was part of a duo. I certainly didn't ask them to, nor was I aware of sending out practically-married-lady vibes. But in retrospect, when you get serious with someone, there's some major circling of the wagons that takes place, and that can shut out even the best friendships. My Formerly friend Melissa (who has three kids under six, so she's barely alive) said it took her a few years to adjust to being married; she felt that her allegiance had to be to her relationship with her husband and that she needed to wall off her marriage for it to feel central. "When Ben and I were first married, it was like, No one can ever know if we have a fight. I was embarrassed," she says.

She nailed exactly what I experienced: If women's friendships are built on shared emotions and commiserations, and you're not talking about what is now the most central relationship in your life, you're not going to feel as close to friends. Paul and I were just married and back in New York from our honeymoon in the summer of 2001, right before the planes hit the World Trade Center. He and I had very different ways of dealing with 9/11. I was frozen with anxiety and grief, jittery and fragile and I didn't know where I could rest my gaze. Certainly not on the TV screen; I couldn't bear to watch the footage of the planes hitting the towers (I still cannot), let alone in a 24-hour loop, as was on the news for weeks after it happened. Paul, on the other hand, was contained and logical and seemed to feel that the more information he had and the more news he absorbed, the better. He met my emotions with facts meant to reassure me, mostly about the relative odds of a repeat occurrence, our pissant Brooklyn block being an unlikely target, and how all the stepped-up security made New York City the safest place in the universe right then. I didn't find it soothing. He didn't get my reaction and I didn't get his. We couldn't comfort each other very well, which put a huge strain on our fledgling marriage.

I did discuss how I felt with my girlfriends, even how Paul

and I weren't connecting on this subject, but I remember choosing my words with care so as not to paint Paul as in any way less than the ideal husband. If my friends saw him as callous or even simply someone who didn't get me, I felt, they might think I was hasty in marrying him, or they might hold it against him, neither of which I wanted. They probably wouldn't have, but my marriage felt too new to risk it. What my self-editing meant, however, was that my friends couldn't appreciate what was upsetting me, and couldn't be supportive.

Dishing about a boyfriend, of course, is one thing. If it isn't serious, it almost feels like sport; those conversations often end in your friend advising you to dump him. Speaking about private things that involve your husband, particularly when you're newly married, feels like a betrayal. That's why many women, myself included, find the first years of marriage to be a bit isolating, even lost years, in terms of our friendships. If things aren't hunky-dory—and in case you haven't heard, marriage is freakin' hard, even when things are good—and you're not talking about it with your friends, you have no idea if they're having the same issues, which makes laying yourself bare even riskier.

But just because your friendships take a backseat to your marriage early on doesn't mean you need those friendships any less. In fact, if you're married, you may well need your friends even more than when you were single. That's because friends come through with a different kind of support than your family—a less invested, more you-centric type of support. Of course, your friends care that you're making decent choices, but they're not as personally affected by your choices, so in the end, whatever makes you happy, they'll find a way to get behind. Not necessarily so, your nearest and dearest.

Let's say I wanted to become a midlife stripper, determined to show the world more and more of me, just as cultural norms and people's near-universal preference would dictate that I reveal less and less. For the record, I think that my becoming a stripper would be awful for everyone involved, but Paul is very supportive so I don't have an example of anything I truly want to do that he has disapproved of.

So let's pretend snaking my fish-white mom body up and down a pole is an aspiration of mine. I'd go to my friends and excitedly and convincingly frame it as an exercise in positive body image: The mass worship I'd get for flaunting my Formerly form would maybe make me feel "empowered" as a woman, which I've seen certain strippers interviewed on TV claim is the true payoff, not the cash tucked into their G-strings. I could sock away that off-the-books G-string green for my kids' college fund, of course, and I'd maybe tap into my sexual core, whatever that is, which would no doubt enhance my intimate relationship with my husband. If nothing else, I'd have more to write about, as if there weren't enough stripper memoirs out there to keep the hellfires burning for eternity.

Then I'd assure them I was serious, and ask what they thought. Some friends would raise an eyebrow and suggest selling pencils from a tin cup outside the Empire State Building might be a more reliable revenue stream. But if it was obvious that I was jazzed about the plan, at least a couple of the more outré would say, *Sure. If it will make you happy, go for it! It's more remunerative than an advanced degree, and possibly aerobic.*

His in-theory support being tested, Paul, of course, would vote a loud no, out of concern for my safety and dignity, his career, what his parents would think and perhaps because he'd see it as evidence of our profound incompatibility. My girls wouldn't like it, either; streaking is a joy for them, but the sight of my mature booty ducking into the shower elicits shrieks of "Eeewww, mushy!" They are just a couple of years away from being mortified by everything I do, and stripping would be worse than even my singing Go-Go's songs as I drop them off at school (they already hate that).

The bottom line is that as a familied Formerly, you don't always have the support of those closest to you to do what you want or need to do. In this fictitious example, my family's happiness is directly dependent on my remaining clothed. And that's totally fair. But that leaves Formerlies like me back in the situation we were when we lived with our parents: negotiating with people who may not feel as we do, and who have a say in what we do. Remember how your 'rents had their own feelings about your donating your college fund to free Tibet and becoming a cranial sacral masseuse? You really needed your friends then, whether you went to college or not, if only for empathy. All stripper silliness aside, there may be times when my husband and kids won't like what I need to do and I will need to do it anyway. It will be so important to have my friends' support.

Many paired-off Formerlies seem to get this, which may be why our friendships are so rewarding—they remind us that we exist separately from our families, as we did in our previous incarnations. Melissa says her Formerly friendships are the best she's had since before she was married. Her marriage is now a fact of her life, not something that feels new and sacred, like it needs to be encased in glass lest it gets covered with greasy fingerprints. "It doesn't feel as private and primal as it once did, like no one can know that we had a fight," she says. "Now I know it's nothing to be embarrassed about, that all my friends have struggles with their spouses, with motherhood, with the balancing act. It feels like we're living the same lives. Even though I see them less, it reminds me of when we were all single and freaking out about being single."

And speaking of single, obviously not all Formerlies are part of a pair. If you're not—by choice or by default—you might, like my friend Rhonda, find yourself counting quite a few non-Formerlies among your friends. This is, of course, because single people may also be child-free, which means they can actually leave their homes after dark and meet up for dinner or drinks or (gasp!) both, even when it's not their birthday. Younger people are likewise able to do this, plus you might just plain have more in common with them than you do with someone who talks about poopy diapers like it's not totally gross. Rhonda is one of my closest friends and Auntie Rhonda to my girls. We spend loads of time together, often with my kids. But if my girls weren't mine, I don't think I'd want to stick around for chicken nuggets with us and call it a rockin' Saturday night, either. We are each other's road not taken.

Talking to Rhonda about hanging with her younger friends made me realize I don't have any non-Formerly friends. Everyone I come into meaningful contact with is a Formerly. Like living in a relatively homogeneous community in which everyone shares your religious or political outlook, it's comfortable and easy to assume a certain foundation of understanding. So when I do on occasion have a real conversation with an adult in her, say, late 20s, everything goes along just fine until I say something that earns me a blank stare. That's my signal that I used a catchphrase or made reference to something that is so anachronistic as to have moved beyond lame to completely irrelevant, thus highlighting the vast generational divide between us. It's worse if you try to explain yourself. Once I found myself singing the Enjoli perfume song (" 'I can bring home the bacon, fry it up in a pan . . .' I'm sure it's on YouTube!") to a tableful of dumbstruck hipsters who so wished I'd stop. I really wanted to. I just couldn't.

To be sure, Rhonda sometimes feels a bit out of sync with her non-Formerly friends, but she loves that they've actually heard Lady Gaga's music, not just her name. "Sometimes I look around and am one of the older people in the bar," says Rhonda, who is 42. "How I feel about it depends on my mood." Sometimes she's a bit wistful; Rhonda watches the ritual hair tosses and wingman maneuvers and cock blocks and women pretending to receive texts from boyfriends waiting at home who don't exist. "Once in a while I wish I could have those moments and chances again," she says, experiencing them for the first time as a young person. On the other hand, she has the wisdom and experience to know that she doesn't have to put up with the insecurity and will-he-call awfulness of dating in your 20s. "Sometimes it's like, *Thank God I don't have to endure this just because everyone expects me to. If I'm not having fun, I can just go home!*"

Right. Would it have killed someone to tell me that I was free to go home at any time, back when I was in my 20s? Then again, I should have been able to figure it out. I was a smart young woman with two feet and subway fare. Why did I think there was some rule that said I had to stay until the last loser had fallen off the bar stool, because that's what I was "supposed" to be doing at my age? I can remember feeling bored and annoyed at so many parties, but laughing a little too loudly and pretending to have "the BEST time!" afraid to leave because I thought I'd miss something. This was my youth! What if "the time of my life" took place right after I left? I felt like all my friends were in on some big joke or vital nugget of information that gave them the appropriate amount of youthful insouciance, while I was, as often as not, worried that my shoes were wrong.

I am so happy to have that little bit of Formerly wisdom. We *can* go home. We don't have to be friends with toxic, draining people to learn that you don't have to be friends with toxic draining people! If you do that once, it's enough. It's not that different the second time. A Formerly is not friends with someone because your mom went to college with her mom or because you want some of her charisma or popularity to rub off on you or because you can't bear to be alone. What a gigantic relief! When you're younger, "You feel so alienated, you try so hard to fit into a group," says Rhonda. "Now my friendships give me community, but I don't need them to give me my identity." Amen to that, sister.

The other big thing about friendships as a Formerly is that we've had decades to accumulate a vast army of friends, some old, some new. I was in the Brownies when I was a kid, and they taught us to sing that adage "Make new friends, but keep the old; one is silver and the other's gold" in a round. One group of girls started the song, and each subsequent group began the verse just after the previous group had finished singing the word "friends." We were told to enunciate the first word, so the song always sounded to me like "MAKE new friends, MAKE new friends, MAKE new friends . . ." and the whole part about keeping old friends because they were so valuable got drowned out. It was also unclear when, if ever, you were supposed to stop singing. It was like a perpetual loop of a single mantra—MAKE new friends—and could cause a little girl to lose her tiny mind and just want to eat all the Girl Scout cookies she was supposed to be selling.

In any event, no thanks to that song, I've been very fortunate to have kept many of my oldest friends, probably because I've lived in one place most of my life, a place (New York City) where people don't automatically flee as soon as they get their driver's licenses. (This may be because many never get their driver's licenses, but that's another subject entirely.) I know it's rare to have so many childhood friends, because my newer friends often marvel at my vintage friendships.

But because I have such a crop of old and relatively new friends, I've got some perspective on why they're both important. Gold and silver is way too facile a way of viewing their absolute and relative value.

Old friends, on the one hand, are the keepers of your context. They knew you when you were your Formerly—whether you were Formerly Hot, Formerly Wild, Formerly Arrogant, Formerly Fat or Formerly Cripplingly Shy but nonetheless the girl who would take down a no-neck fraternity bully with one cutting phrase if you had to. No matter what you become, they get it, they get you and they get how you arrived at now. What's more, if you stray too far from what you were, in a bad way—say, you're Patrick Dempsey, all sexy and sensitive as McDreamy on *Gray's Anatomy*—and you get a swelled head, you need an old friend around to remind you that in 1986, you once considered yourself lucky to star in *Meatballs III*.

Then again, if your Formerly wasn't something you were entirely proud of, new friends can be a fresh start. They don't know you as Formerly Slutty, that girl who slept with half the guys in her freshman dorm, or Formerly the Prodigy, the one who everyone thought would be the first woman President but who now works in a yarn store (So the eff what? You love to knit!). They see who you are now, and like what they see, and don't have lingering judgments.

Of course, newer friends can't see patterns, a perspective that as a Formerly I need more than ever. With so little spare time, I find myself ever more frustrated when I make the same dumb-ass mistakes I've made for years, or get all twisted up over the things in life that will probably never change and are just not worth the angst. It's good to have a friend who has been around long enough to say, "And you're *surprised* that your stepmother wants you to fly across the country with your toddler and infant at great expense and sleep in a motel over a holiday weekend when it would be much easier for she and your dad to come to you? Why? Because she's always been so accommodating? Remember the time when . . ." It is so validating and makes you feel ever so much less like a crazy lady. And if a new friend steps in with a fresh way to talk to the difficult stepmother (since muttering "I hate you!" under your breath since you were 16 hasn't worked), all the better. New friends let you make new patterns—they let you see that if you act differently, maybe you'll get different results.

Either way, you've got two great girls to go out to a bar with once in a while. You can order a silly-sounding drink, blow off some steam for as long as you can keep your eyes open and remember you're not old. That is, if you can ever find a date to meet up that works for all three of you.

4

Friends Every Formerly Needs

1. *The blunt but loving friend.* She'll tell you, yes, your skin is looking a little slack these days, but it's nothing a decent night cream, a little microdermabrasion and a good night's sleep won't cure.

2. *The outraged-on-your-behalf friend.* "WTF? Are they *trying* to make things harder for us? Would it kill them to make a bikini top with an underwire? It's not you—it's the ⋆^&⋆ bathing suit. Christ."

3. *The friend who will wipe your kid's ass as if it were her own kid's ass.* This is the same friend who also really won't hold it against you if your kid pukes on her rug, and will take him home from school with her kid if your sitter bails and you're stuck at work, because she knows your boss is itching to replace you with some recent grad who he can pay half of what you make. 'Nuff said.

4. *The friend who can tell you which celebrity has had what work done.* Some people have an eagle eye for this and I find it incredibly helpful to be reminded that—despite protestations that all they do is drink a lot of water, wear sunscreen and hike for 20 minutes with their dogs and that's why they have unlined faces and fat-free bodies— no one looks like Nicole Kidman and Angelina Jolie at their age with their offspring without a little high-tech help.

5. *The friend who reminds you to trust your gut.* Formerlies know that their instincts are usually right, but the transition from what you were to a Formerly can be destabilizing. It helps to have someone around who points out that whatever choice you make will turn out to be the right one, because one way or another, you'll make it so.

. . . And Friends for Whom Formerlies Have No Use

1. The friend who is deeply hurt and thinks you would already know why if you were really her friend.
2. The friend who can't even pretend to like your significant other and/or who can't genuinely like your children.
3. The friend who points out that if you eat two Lean Cuisines you may as well have eaten a regular meal.

You're not an idiot. You're a Formerly. You're doing the best you can.

4. The friend who won't come to your neighborhood at least half the time.

5. The friend who remains silent and allows you to believe everything is as easy as she makes it seem.

My Friend Restraint

Formerly needs more than jeans in her closet, of course, but figuring out what works now that you're in a new category of human can be tricky. So every time I go shopping, online or in person, I bring along my personal stylist, Restraint. She sounds like a big old poop, but she's not—in fact, she'll take you clubbing, and you'll have a rockin' time, but the next day you won't be nearly dead of a hangover and hallucinating that you did it with one of the Ramones.

Here's an example of her type of thinking: Wear a mini-skirt if you want. But don't wear it with fishnets *and* platform pumps *and* a bustier *and* an MC jacket. With black tights, a fitted blazer and flats, you're good. Restraint says I can pretty much wear whatever I want, and no single item is off-limits. I just don't want to look like I'm dressing up like a teenager for Halloween, and Restraint helps me make that determination. What's more, too much of any single thing on your person at any given time—whether it's leather, se-

quins, Lily Pulitzer prints, self-tanner or Swarovski crystals—
is no good. This is true for anyone of any age or life stage,
but becomes even more important when you get to be a
Formerly and can no longer wear wrist loads of bracelets *and*
big hoop earrings *and* lots of rings without looking like a
fortune-teller.

Restraint also guides me well when it comes to trends.
She basically says to wink at a trend and maybe flirt a little,
but no making out and certainly no full body contact.
Whereas before, I might have embraced a trend—say, full-on
vintage 1950s Doris Day—by donning a poofy, nip-waist
cocktail dress, bright red lipstick, pointy pumps and a handbag made out of wicker, now I'll stick with my own look
and maybe wave hello to Doris across the party (I'll get just
the wicker handbag, or just the pumps, but not the whole
getup).

I see a parallel between the way I conducted my romantic
life pre-Formerly and the way I shopped then. When I was
single (which was until I was 34 and was on the verge of
Formerlydom), I felt if a guy was nice or smart or interesting or came highly recommended, I should at least give him
a chance. I was looking for love, and I didn't know enough
about myself to be sure of exactly what I needed in a partner, so I tried a lot of guys on, as it were. Over time, through
trial and error and making the same mistake 12 or 30 times,
I figured out what I needed, what I wanted and what I could
live with. I also knew what I couldn't tolerate, under any circumstances. This narrowed my field and eventually I found

the "style" of guy that works for me. The one I eventually fell in love with and married fits in squarely with that style. Similarly, I tried a myriad of clothing styles and followed trends over the years until I developed a sense of what worked and what didn't.

(I'm oversimplifying, of course. I dated the guy equivalent of blister-producing, toe-crushing pointy masochist stilettos way longer than was wise, and rolled my eyes at some well-made classics that I probably should have tried when I had the chance. But you get the idea.)

Knowing what works for you—in all aspects of your life, including relationships and fashion—is one of the fantastic things about being a Formerly. "You finally have some perspective on yourself," says my friend Alex, a fashion writer and fabulous Formerly living in France (Paris, natch!). "You have seen yourself in photos for 20 years, with five or six different hair trends, living through the preppy era, the punk era, etc. In that time, you come to realize, *There's a bigger me than all of these fleeting outfits and styles and moods and trends.* As you get older and become a Formerly, you have a sense of yourself as more permanent than any of those things. That makes you a bit less of a fashion victim."

I totally agree. When I pick up *Elle* or *Vogue,* and am enlightened as to what's "in," it's a variation on something I've seen, and likely worn before. I know whether or not it works for me. *Oh, look! Blue-and-white-striped shirts and wide-leg pants—they're dusting off the nautical theme. I could never pull off that whole cute first-mate bit. Peasant dresses and gauzy blouses?*

Right. Boho chic. That I can work with. Shopping is a much calmer, less compulsive experience. "The big jeans that I wore in the '90s with the paper-bag waist—they didn't look good on me," says Alex. "They've come back around again, like everything does. Sure, this time they are in a lighter fabric, with a higher waist, but it's the same thing. I'm like, nope. I know not to mess with that, because I have some wisdom. All that other stuff, it's fleeting."

As for me, let's see . . . I'm wisely steering clear of fluorescent colors, jeans with zippers on the tapered legs, T-shirts with block capital letters shouting "RELAX!" and anything that has been made to look distressed with a grain thresher or doused with acid.

I'm not saying that I need to wear the same thing year after year with no variation (and no fun) and now that I've found my style I aim to be buried in it. I'm just thinking it through before I throw myself like a fashion slut at every trend that looks my way.

The whole vintage thing is a big mess now that I'm old enough to have actually lived through some of the eras being ironically re-referred to in fashion. Part of what makes vintage clothing so excellent is the contrast between the age of the outfit and the age of the person wearing it. A 20-year-old hipster boy wearing '70s polyester or a 30-year-old going a little *Mad Men* is hot. A 42-year-old woman wearing a fringed suede vest, a paisley blouse and bell-bottoms? Cue the ballad of the sad clown. It's time to put those clothes back in the Salvation Army clothing pool and let some young chick discover the 1970s for the first time. She'll think she invented it. It'll be sweet.

Retro irony in general, Restraint says, should be left to those who didn't actually eat Froot Loops as part of a balanced breakfast when Toucan Sam was still the Bruce Springsteen of cereal mascots. That means Formerlies such as myself are wise to avoid T-shirts with Sam, Mr. Bubble or Wonder Woman on them. Your own youth can be nostalgic, but only other people's childhoods can be ironic. Oh, and I implore you to share this with any male Formerlies in your life. If he still has that Stones T-shirt from the *Tattoo You* tour and it miraculously still fits, he should feel free to wear it. But kindly discourage him from going to the Virgin Megastore and buying the reissue of the tee from a concert he once attended. That makes me want to cry. If his T-shirt looks 30 years younger than he is—because it is—there's something tragic about the whole endeavor. He knows he was at the concert. It ought to be OK if no one else does unless it comes up naturally in conversation. It's also OK to handcuff him to the radiator, if that's what it takes to stop him from getting the shirt. Even if he doesn't thank you for it, you're still right.

6

Unpopular Culture

didn't want to get my daughters the American Girl dolls in the first place, mainly because they cost north of $100 apiece, and there was no predicting whether they'd wind up wedged between the bed and the wall like so many please-oh-please must-have toys before them. "No way. Not a chance," I said. But even as the words left my lips I had a feeling I was going to cave.

Sure enough, as fast as you can say, "Accessories sold separately," I did. I was no match for the instinctively manipulative campaign of cuteness my ladies launched. To save face (and money), I told them that (okay, okay!) if they could convince their grandparents to spring for them, I'd bestow my reluctant consent. The grandparents acquiesced, as grandparents are programmed to do.

In truth, by the time we were to place the online order, I was reluctantly grooving on the dolls, in particular the historical series. For those not familiar with the American Girl industrial complex, along with modern ones on skateboards with little schoolbags, they have a line of dolls of various ethnicities from different eras in American history, for which you can get storybooks, costumes and other accoutrements. There was Felicity, the one Vivian wanted, a plucky, horse-loving rebel growing up in colonial Virginia; Addy, an escaped slave, and Josefina, a Mexican-American from the southwest of the 1820s. I noticed some dolls from the 20th century, too, such as Rebecca, a Russian-Jewish immigrant in 1914 New York, and Kit Kittredge, the spunky Depression-era reporter who Abigail Breslin played in the movie. Each came with a book about what it was like to be a little girl during her period in history. At least American Girl dolls are educational, I thought. Plus, they don't have those poofed-up blow-job lips or wear hoochie outfits like the Bratz dolls my girls also crave.

I was talking with my friend Marisa about Felicity et al., and she mentioned that one of her daughters had the Julie Albright doll. I said I didn't know about Julie; was she from the historical series?

"Oh, yes," Marisa answered grimly. "She's from 1974."

Nineteen seventy-four? *1974???* Since when are the 1970s a historical era?

Sure, they were several decades ago, but *history,* as in, behind a glass case with a plaque on it at the Smithsonian, no way! The dolls are supposed to be girls of eight or nine. Guess who was around that age in 1974? Formerlies! Uh-huh. Marisa and I were seven in 1974. In the eyes of American Girl, and consequently millions of actual girls all over the country, the children of the 1970s are veritable historical figures who could stand alongside Sacajawea or Elizabeth Cady Stanton on a textbook time line in a history book. "Nineteen twenty: Women won the right to vote. Nineteen forty-five: The United Nations Charter was signed. Nineteen seventy-four: Your mother was seven."

I was appalled, but since Julie Albright had been doing macramé and staging love-ins in Marisa's house for months already, her wound was not as fresh. She just sighed and let me rant. I looked Julie up on the American Girl website. She looks like she just stepped off the *Partridge Family* bus, with long, swishy, blond hair, sporting a white peasant blouse and bell-bottoms, with a braided, beaded leather belt and a crocheted cap. Marisa read the *Meet Julie* book that came with the doll to her daughters before bed the other night. "It talked about Billie Jean King and male chauvinist pigs. Her friend Ivy had a pocketbook made out of old blue jeans and she wore those Buffalo sandals I really wanted but my mom wouldn't let me get! They mentioned mood rings and everything. Am I historical simply because I remember that stuff?"

I sure never thought so, but evidently we are. Did American Girl *really* need to point it out so starkly? They couldn't have done a '60s flower-child doll instead, thus ensuring that little girls could learn about smoking dope and war protesting without insinuating that their moms were "historical"? Thirty seconds with a calculator could have told the American Girl R&D team that women who were girls in the '70s might have children of doll-buying age.

Of course, to a little kid, the 1970s may as well be feudal times. Sasha is always asking me things like, did they have taxis when I was a child, and did I have to make my own cheese, like Laura Ingalls in the Little House books I read to them? To my girls, for whom "the olden days" means any time before they were born, Julie's world is as alien as Felicity's.

Still, I'm the one with the credit card, not Sasha. I would not have had a problem with it if they had Julie in a line of dolls called When Mom Was Your Age or some such. When I hear Elton John singing "Bennie and the Jets" and realize that song came out when I was seven, I think, *Sheesh, that was a long time ago.* But it seems gratuitously callous to be relegated to the annals of history in a semi-official capacity by an outside entity while I'm not only still kicking, but kicking ass, thank you very much. Having a doll from one's "historical" era feels like getting a lifetime achievement award, only—how can I say this clearly—I'M NOT THAT OLD!

Harumph.

These days, it often seems as if the main purpose of popular culture is to remind me of my age. But it wasn't always so. When I was a kid, I listened to Carly Simon's "You're So Vain" time and again, wailing into my hairbrush. I got a huge thrill out of the line "I'll bet you think this song is about you, Don't you, don't you?" Simon was accusing the subject of the song of having a swelled head, while at that very moment, she was singing to HIM! Get it? The song *was* about him! I felt so smart, so in on the joke. Cut me a break. I was seven. It was 1974. I'm told that's ancient history.

That song, preceded by an abiding love for Ernie and Bert, was my introduction to the prolonged bear hug that is popular culture. I hugged back. I loved belonging to the community it created, and quickly found that listening to a person's thoughts about the songs and ads and TV shows and movies that were lobbed at us with the speed and accuracy of a pitching machine provided a tidy shortcut into her head. What someone thought was cool, as well as whether she disavowed what she truly enjoyed in favor of what she was *supposed* to think was cool, told me a lot about how she saw herself. And thanks to the dizzying array of media (it seemed dizzying to me, even pre-cable and pre-Internet) I could chat with anyone, in the old-fashioned sense of the verb. Even on a torturous blind date in my 20s with the insurance industry lobbyist nephew of my stepfather's college roommate, we shared a mutual bewilderment that Ace of Base was as popular as they apparently were. It didn't a love match make, but the subject was our life raft until the check came.

Somewhere along the line, the bear released me from his hug. Now that I'm a Formerly, the song is most definitively NOT about me, a 42-year-old mom of two for whom it would be a bit pervy to cop to a favorite Jonas (Nick). I remember when I was but ten and even I knew that Lynyrd Skynyrd was a band, not a person. My mom, of course, did not, and earned an exaggerated eye roll from yours truly. Today's Formerlies tend to be more plugged in than our moms were, but as you read this, I am positive that somewhere a Formerly is asking her kid if Franz Ferdinand is that nice boy in school who wore the lederhosen on International Heritage Day. That will be me as soon as my girls start liking music that didn't originate on the Disney Channel. (I'll save you having to Google it: Franz Ferdinand is not an individual but a Scottish band about which those who are not yet Formerlies are all atwitter, no pun intended. I only know this because someone mentioned them and I had to fake recognition until I could go Google.)

The songs that *are* about me, or at one time were, are either being sung at hugely hyped reunion tours at stadiums across the nation, are being used in commercials for casino resorts, or to entice me to order the surf and turf for $9.99 at T.G.I. Friday's. I get it now: Being a Formerly in pop cultural terms means that the sound track of your life is now playing on the lite rock stations, in the Sunday Night Oldies lineups or, if you've managed to keep an ear open to the semi-current, on the adult contemporary stations. You might hear a Muzak-ified version of songs you know while you're waiting on hold with your cable provider, but you won't hear it when you go into Forever 21 to get a gift card for your 19-year-old babysitter's birthday. There, you will feel like an overstimulated old person. It will all seem too loud and discordant (even though some of the clothes are cute) and you will probably consider walking out and just writing your babysitter a check.

My own musical tastes were arrested sometime in my 20s. My theory on this is that all through high school and college, you are basically one gigantic, living, breathing, studying, angsting, Dorito-eating adolescent raw nerve ending, hooking up and getting your heart broken and learning that you were breathtakingly wrong about all that you thought you knew. That jacked-up feeling of betrayal and urgency and intensity is matched by songs about the same issues that you hear on the radio. It feels as if Tracy Chapman or Alanis Morissette or Depeche Mode have crawled up your brain stem into your head and are shouting out everything you couldn't possibly express because you're not as talented as they are. They get it! They get you! That's what makes it "your" music.

Fast-forward to now. When someone asks me how I'm doing, and I stop to think beyond the knee-jerk "Fine," my answer is usually something like, "You know, good, thanks for asking." If I think the person really wants to hear about my life, I might add that I'm busy or stressed or tired and offer a few unthrilling details as to why, but that everyone's healthy and nothing is horribly wrong right this second, so overall, I'm giving today a thumbs-up. Aside from the occasional miracle of birth or unexpected crisis, life is on an even keel and my fondest wish on an average day is for an extra hour's sleep and more time to spend with the people I love. If I find I've dropped a few pounds without trying or discover a forgotten $20 in the pocket of the jeans I just pulled out of the dryer, it's time to break out the margarita mix.

Now, imagine trying to set any of that to music; stability and contentment don't make for great lyrics. Neither does compromise, a rendezvous with your mortgage broker about refinancing or a passive-aggressive phone conversation with your spouse about who will stop for baby wipes on the way home. I could see it as a country song, albeit not a very good one.

But you know what? I'd much rather turn on the radio and feel a wee bit left out than still be living the kind of life people write songs about, at least the songs that have to do with alienation and cheating and that deep-seated fucked-upness in a lover that can be mistaken for depth when you're young and figuring it all out. Drama and upheaval are not constants in my life as they were when I was younger, and the relative stillness has let me revel in what I've built instead of constantly sweeping up after it's been blown to bits.

"Our Lips Are Sealed" by the Go-Go's is on my iPod, and I blasted it for my daughters in the car the other night. I squawked along with the lyrics, "Can you hear them, they talk about us, telling lies, well that's no surprise." The girls loved it and wanted to hear it 30 times in a row as they always do, which kind of killed it for me ("But Mommy, could you please not sing this time?"). On the 29th go-round, I realized that I no longer do anything titillating enough for "them," whoever they are, to bother talking about, let alone lying about. I used to at least *think* I did. I see young women on the street now who have an air of being the center of attention, which of course makes them the center of attention. They step off the curb expecting traffic to stop, and it does! If I stepped off the curb now, traffic would probably stop because no one likes a lawsuit, but not because the drivers and I are all in agreement that because I'm young and invincible I own the road. What's more, I probably wouldn't step off the curb and take the chance that the driver wasn't too busy texting to notice me and step on the brake.

I do not miss being the center of attention—it's a lot of pressure, actually—but I do miss feeling relevant. If there ever was a "them," people I didn't know who might nonetheless be interested in my comings or goings or thoughts or feelings, I am now 100 percent certain that "they" couldn't care less. My friends and family, of course, remain interested in my point of view, and occasionally someone who is marketing a butter substitute or a new depression medication may ask me to fill out a survey. But I no longer have a sense that what I or my friends do is of vital interest, that it represents a rumbling under the surface of society that some writer might notice and remark upon as indicative of a new, potentially significant wave of thought. Mind you, it wasn't as if I was called upon for my blinding insights on a **regular** basis, but I felt in-the-mix enough that if asked, I could add to the dialogue. Now I am simply off the radar of relevance.

But now that I'm over the shock of being seen as irrelevant by the nebulous "them," it's no big deal. Most of the time, many younger people, especially the hip ones, seem to me overly conscious that they're being talked about, which strikes me as more energy than I want to devote to such things. The less I think about what "they" think of me, the more time I have to think about what will make me and those who matter to me happy. Being a Formerly might look a teensy bit boring, if the observer applies only a cursory glance, the same kind of cursory glance that determines that a woman is no longer hot if she's older. But from where I sit, there's nothing boring about being a Formerly. And "they" won't know that until they get to be one themselves.

All this being said, I'm not completely hopeless when it comes to current music. If a song is a national phenomenon or gets the Christian right all worried that our children are being recruited as lesbians, it'll penetrate my distracted, disorganized consciousness. Still, by and large, the only things on the new music stations that sound familiar to me are the snippets of "old school" tunes that are sampled within the new releases. I'll hear a Michael Jackson riff or the backbeat from a Grandmaster Flash song and for a second my heart leaps—*I actually know that one! Check me out!* Then the singer's unfamiliar voice returns, and I see it was just a tease. Later, when the 20-year-old rapper appears on *Live! with Regis and Kelly* (what he's doing on that show I have no idea, but then again, I'm watching it, and I have no idea why) I'll find out that the stanza I knew was included because it was by his mom's favorite artist.

Television is a bit easier to stay up on than music and

movies, especially because I'm often too pooped to go out in the evenings, and the advent of DVR technology means I never have to miss an episode of *The Office* or *Mad Men*. As a Formerly, I'm included in that pocket of pop culture—even targeted, because I presumably have money to spend on BMWs and FedEx and the other stuff that's advertised during the breaks. (Hey! Is that Queen and David Bowie singing "Under Pressure" on that Propel water commercial? Why, I know that song! And coincidentally, I'm suddenly parched. . . .)

My friend Josie, who has been in bands since she could bang two pots together, takes it especially hard when one of her counterculture icons starts shilling for corporate America. Swiffer tends to score the best of old-school pop, but the list is endless. To name just a few, you can hear Iggy Pop for Royal Caribbean Cruise Lines, Digable Planets for Tide and Squeeze for Dentyne gum. I get why Josie finds it disheartening, but we've all done things we never thought we'd do (mini-van with built-in DVD player, anyone?). I don't think you can blame an aging rocker for wanting to cash in on a past hit. People have to eat, especially Iggy Pop.

What gets *me* is that Madison Avenue seems to think we Formerlies are soooo easy—and evidently we are! It galls me that I am, in fact, more likely to be favorably disposed toward a product if I associate it with a cool tune from an era when I was cooler than I am now. It's like crying at an obvious tearjerker—you feel manipulated and a little idiotic, while at the same time validated, if in a backhanded way. *I know, let's get these ladies to associate our vile, smelly de-pilatory with a time in their lives when they weren't working 55 hours a week and then coming home to follow a child and a dog around with a sponge before collapsing in bed with still-hairy legs. If the song speaks to them, they'll unthinkingly grab it as they shop in their usual harried fugue state.* The songs in these ads still speak to me. It's just that before, when a song like The Cure's "Pictures of You" spoke to me, it said, *How precious and ephemeral is love.* Now it says, *Run out and buy an HP printer.* (Yes, I own an HP printer.)

I'm beginning to understand that the pop cultural divide between a Formerly and someone who is not is vast, and is as much of a marker of the passage of time as any facial wrinkle or income bracket. Our facility with computers, of course, is a big, thick line in the sand between Formerlies and those that were born later. Formerlies are once again "tweens" vis-à-vis computer technology: too old to have been immersed in it when our brains were soft and ab-sorbent, and too young to ignore it entirely, at least if we want to earn a living and function in society.

Occasionally I run into a (usually male) Formerly who still thinks it's kind of neat that he is not charmed by tech-nology, and proudly declares himself a luddite. (The original Luddites, of course, being artisans in Britain at the start of the Industrial Revolution who felt they were being replaced by the advent of machines and so sometimes torched textile factories.) Nowadays, it strikes me as plain lame: There's noth-ing cool or intellectual about not knowing how to do something. The IT guys sure don't want to hear about it and I highly doubt it will get you laid.

When I was in college, few people had their own computers, and if they did, they were awkward, hulking behemoths with tiny glowing amber screens, and people had to bring their floppy discs elsewhere to print things out on that paper with the holes on the sides. There was something called a computer lab, but I never went there, having heard horror stories about senior theses vanishing into the ether just hours before they were due. People only a few years younger than us had computers in high school, but my contemporaries and I typed our papers.

I'm not proud, but even today, after years of using Macs and PCs for work and muddling through a blogging program for formerlyhot.com, my first instinct when I get that spinning rainbow beach ball of death (Mac users will know what I mean) is to smack the monitor, take a nap and hope that the problem resolves by the time I get up. There's a chance I'd be that way even if I had my first keyboard to drool on when I was a toddler, like my daughters did.

But for the longest time, the sense of not knowing enough on a basic level to address even the most minor problem myself made me want to scream with despair. Sometimes I'd go to the "help" menu and find that I lacked even the vocabulary to look up my problem—"the little hand thingy won't turn back into the arrow thingy" wasn't in the index. It felt like I was being asked to learn an entirely new language, one that I didn't have the time for, and one that would not enable me to order delicious food in a foreign country.

I've gotten more adept through sheer exposure, but even now, decades after MS-DOS, when something goes wrong in a big way, and I'm told that there is a new driver (I have no idea what that is) I can download to prevent the problem from occurring in the future, I feel like smacking the monitor again, because I know I will need help even with that. I hate feeling like I'm not adept at what has become as integral a part of daily life as putting a key into a lock and turning it.

A Formerly friend of mine, Rachel, who runs a magazine website, did make me feel a lot better about my tech reticence, though. "I started at a website at a time when no one knew what they were talking about," she said. "I saw behind the curtain, so I know that it all started as a bunch of people totally making it up." To an extent, that's what's still going on, which is probably why there's an "update" every few weeks that you need to avail yourself of. Granted, Rachel is technically inclined, but her attitude—that there's no way to know everything, so you shouldn't feel bad if you don't—is one I'd be wise to apply to anything that feels like I'm too much of a Formerly to dip into.

But don't for a minute think that I'm an Andy Rooney–like dinosaur who can muse for an entire segment about how many wristwatches I own but never wear or who asks for my emails to be printed out for me so I can read them in hard copy. Unlike the stereotype of folks my mom's age, I'm not fearful or dismissive of technology, even if I don't see it as the extension of self that younger people often do. The problem is, I am barely able to find the time and the presence of mind to learn what I need to know to make the technology I already have do the minimal things I ask it to do, let alone explore the next generation of gizmo and all of its many features, the ones that the guy at the store assured me I could have so much fun with.

Fun. Hah! Let's say I somehow miraculously have four hours budgeted for fun—fun for me primarily, not fun for the kids that will also be enjoyable for me. There are about 700 things I'd spend that time doing before learning how to use a new handheld device that I will probably drop in a Portosan at a Cheetah Girls concert. Coffee and a pedicure with a girlfriend I haven't seen in months; a massage and a leisurely trawl at a bookstore; seeing a movie with my husband that's not by Disney/Pixar. You get the idea. That's another way you know you're a Formerly: if you simply want your gadgets to do the three or five things you need them to do and do them properly.

Of course, there are tech-minded Formerlies who are interested in technology for technology's sake, just as I'm into clothes beyond the fact that they cover my naked body. And I love that, in part because they can explain it all to me when I'm about to smack my computer. But I'll always be clawing my way up the learning curve. All of this technology made its appearance when I was already a grown-up and had everything well in hand. It basically stood there like a stubborn child with its lip out and insisted I drop everything and learn how to use it. In the early 1990s, someone who didn't check with me first decided that cassette tapes were no longer good enough and that everyone had to convert to CDs. Remember that? It seems quaint now, but aside from a gnarled mess of an overplayed love mix from a high school boyfriend, I didn't understand why I had to go out and buy CDs of the same music I already owned. Now that there's a new thingy I supposedly must upgrade to every other week, you can see as I might be a bit annoyed.

One could argue that another sign you are a Formerly is the degree to which you are thrown for a loop when websites you like are "upgraded" beyond recognition. My Formerly friend Melissa O., who ran the site for a magazine I used to work for (but nonetheless is stymied at having to make a conference call, which makes me perversely happy), says that after a redesign, people Formerly age and older are less likely to come back. "Even if the site is better and easier and clearer, she's thinking, I can't find that one thing I used to love to do. A teenager will take the time to visit again and explore."

Well, exactly. Not only does that teenager have far more time to screw around on the Internet looking for neat sites than I do, but if surfing the web is not part of a Formerly's job or something she finds relaxing, odds are, she's online to stay in touch and do her business. I mainly go online to read news and blogs, to shop and to get information for stories that I'm working on. The only pure fun I have is on the massive timesuck that is Facebook. And predictably enough, when they redid their site after I'd been on for a few months, I felt like someone had come into my house, rearranged my underwear drawer, hidden all my everyday bras and panties and replaced them with wedgie-inducing thongs and impractical lingerie that was for someone with boobs that stayed up all on their own anyway and so didn't need it.

I whined about it a fair amount (on Facebook, of course, because there was no way I was going to learn how to use another social networking site) and many Formerlies agreed with me. Others accused us of being resistant to change, and told us to get over it. They weren't wrong. I did sort of feel like I was turning into my grandparents. They're gone now, but they used to become terribly anxious when their routines were disrupted. I kind of understood why even when I was a kid: They'd lived long enough to know what worked for them, and they didn't relish any added challenges. When the little things, like getting in and out of your gigantic mauve aircraft carrier of a Lincoln becomes more difficult, some valet changing your radio station can be unnerving. Until you find the Perry Como station again, it feels like someone has fucked with your sense of reality just a little bit. And if the Publix runs out of your favorite brand of gluten-free dinner rolls, that can knock you flat on your ass for a good half hour, and require a therapeutic rehash (or several) with your wife of 50-plus years.

I'm not set in my ways to the degree that my Lincolndriving, Florida-living, gluten-free-roll-eating, Loehmann's-shopping, Bronx-transplanted grandparents were. But I've got enough on my plate that when the things that are supposed to be relaxing require that I read instructions, I get cranky. It took me fully three months to not miss the "old" Facebook, and then they changed it on me again. I know I'm supposed to roll with it, but becoming a Formerly is change enough for now.

7

Formerly Famous

As long as there have been TV sitcoms, there has been the goofy TV dad trying to appear cool for his kids by using ridiculously dated catchphrases, or rendering current catchphrases ridiculous simply by virtue of the fact that he's using them. The can't-miss message is, once you're a Formerly, you should stop saying things like "It's da bomb," "Fierce!" or, worse, "Talk to the hand," because you're only highlighting the convention center–sized gap between you and the young person you're trying to connect with.

I'm simply not in contact with enough cool people to even pretend to keep up. The fact that what's cutting edge in technology and music and film and catchphrases seems to turn over much more frequently than when we were in our 20s and 30s might just be that phenomenon of time seeming to pass more quickly when you're older, or perhaps it really is spinning that fast—black, white and red all over like a penguin in a blender.

Still, the first time it hits you that you are on the outside of pop culture looking in, it can be startling. Here's what happened to my friend Kathleen, who is a political consultant. Last year, Kathleen was checking out a video Nancy Pelosi's office posted on YouTube. Right in the middle of it, the sound of a record needle scratching against vinyl could be heard, and then the unmistakable strains of '80s pop singer Rick Astley singing "Never Gonna Give You Up." Astley himself then made a brief appearance in acid wash doing that little side-to-side hair-floppy '80s dance before the video faded out to a picture of the Capitol, lending the whole thing an air of official dignity and understatement.

Kathleen sat in wonderment. Her cubemate, a man in his 20s who is fond of retro attire, smiled and said, "Shit! Pelosi's been rickrolled!" Kathleen hadn't the foggiest, although of course she remembered the song. "She's been what?" He patiently explained what the term meant: that some wag manages to tape over your YouTube submission with a Rick Astley song. It's a playful form of video vandalism utilizing a washed-up Formerly Famous pop star from the era before there was an Internet. Rickrolling is now what Rick Astley is most famous for, and all he had to do to be resurrected from the Where Are They Now? cold case file was absolutely nothing.

In any event, Kathleen was appalled to find out that the term "rickrolling" has been in widespread use since 2006. "But I pay attention to popular culture," she protested. "I can't believe I've never heard it!" He shrugged and swiveled back to his computer.

I'd never heard of rickrolling, either. But that's not the point. The point is in what Kathleen said: "But I pay attention to popular culture!" You only have to pay attention to pop culture if you are not part of it, if you are on the outside looking in and thus must make a conscious effort to learn it, as if it were Swahili. When you're young, pop culture sinks in through your pores like the UV rays and free radicals that will someday make you look old. What makes you a Formerly is not ignorance of popular culture. It is the initial denial of your ignorance, and then the indignant reaction to your ignorance, because you pride yourself on not being ignorant, goddamn it. As if being a Formerly can be overcome by good, old-fashioned American industriousness.

Which it cannot. To a degree, that ignorance can be diminished somewhat, if you work at it. Whether it's worth the time and effort it takes to stay au courant as a Formerly, when the figurative song just plain isn't about you and there is going to be a new song that isn't about you every week, is a tough call. Few Formerlies have the time, especially if they have children. I used to see a movie a week. Now, whenever there's a movie that sounds good, I go from missing it in the theater to missing it on cable, to having it expire off the DVR before I have a chance to watch it. By the time I remember to get it on Netflix, it's been out over a year, several people have ruined the ending for me and the universe is abuzz about an entirely different film I'll probably not see any time soon.

On the one hand, you want to feel in-the-know enough to be able to discuss things like what's "heating up the blogosphere" and the decline of print media and use words like "app" and know texting acronyms like "IMHFO" without having to look them up (like I did when I first saw it . . . In My Humble Fucking Opinion, in case you were wondering). And of course, you want to employ any technology that will truly make your lunatic life easier. On the other hand, you may just want to close your eyes and wait for the next wave of technology or music or film to wash over you, and maybe ride that one. Or not.

Another option is to band together with other Formerlies and form your own little pop cultural bubble, where the measure of coolness is not whether you have heard the latest cutting-edge band or have the newest application for your iPhone, but the depth of knowledge you retain about the individual members of the cast of *Full House*. Finding that bubble is one of the big reasons I love going onto Facebook, along with discovering that we all worried about the same things in high school, even as we all thought everyone else was living the perfect life. What can I say? I was really sad when Bea Arthur died. There was always Maude and then all of a sudden there wasn't. I hadn't recently thought about the feminist goddess with the long cardigans I watched as a child who set the stage for my mom to grow up and grow a pair and strike out on her own, but I was glad to be able to join a Bea Arthur fan group on Facebook and read about the cool stuff she'd done. If this makes me a loser, I'm fine with that. Apparently I'm in good company.

Whether or not you care that you're largely left out of

pop culture naturally depends on whether you ever valued being in-the-know or relevant in the first place. I did, but as a private citizen. People who were once famous seem to find it unbearable to be so excluded, which is probably why so many of them agree to be on shows like *Celebrity Rehab with Dr. Drew* or the one that was all about Scott Baio and his Peter Pan syndrome. I cannot tear myself away from even well-worn repeats of those VH1 reality shows, the ones in which celebrities who are known for something they accomplished a long time ago interact in front of the cameras like organisms in a petri dish. The format is pretty standard: Place a Formerly Famous person in ludicrously contrived situations with other Formerly Famous people and tape them bonding or else clawing one another's spray tans off in exchange for a chance to get their names out into the public consciousness again (and thus, hopefully, reverse their Formerly status).

The Surreal Life included Erik Estrada from *CHiPs,* the Go-Go's Jane Wiedlin (as cool as you'd think), the late Tammy Faye Messner (cooler than you'd think), Vanilla Ice (even less cool than you'd think), female wrestler Chyna, Charo and many other random folks living in various houses together, trying to demonstrate that they are more than their personas. There is also a Formerly Famous weight-loss show, *Celebrity Fit Club* (on which we learned that the guy who played Screech on *Saved by the Bell* is not a nice person), *Confessions of a Teen Idol* and the low-rent *Bachelor* knockoffs starring Flava Flav from Public Enemy and Poison's Bret

Michaels. On *Rock of Love,* Michaels fondled his way through a throng of grown-up groupies, perpetually surprised that it was so hard to divine which of these large-breasted, scantily clad women calling one another bitches and liars really loves him for *him,* you know?

Ridiculous as they are, I had to ask myself why I watch these shows. I think a big reason is because I want to see how the Formerly Famous trying to regain their fame are coping with getting older. Aside from the fact that being older means you have less time before you die (which, let's face it, sucks), I wouldn't want to be the person I was in my 20s. I've built a better, more fulfilling life now than I ever had when I was young and hot (i.e., considered hot by people who don't already know that I'm beautiful on the inside). I wonder if the celebrities on these shows feel that way? Are they handling getting older any better than I am? With their entirely redone bodies and the fact that they clearly don't have much going on or they wouldn't see shows like these as a good opportunity, they don't seem like the likeliest crew from which to be learning about aging gracefully.

Then again, wisdom often comes from unlikely sources. Staring at the screen has taught me that clinging desperately to what you once were is conduct unbecoming to a Formerly, as is taking yourself too seriously—both are far worse than any wrinkles, even those unsightly hash marks between your eyes that make you look perpetually pissed off. Botox can relax those away if they really bother you. But there is no injectable to help the Formerly who argues with the maître d' at The Ivy that he should get a table near Harvey Weinstein because he was once on *Charles in Charge*. That person is not aging gracefully. The one who wonders how it is that she's about to do a weigh-in on national television with Marcia Brady, laughs and does it anyway is, in my view, getting older with the right attitude.

Aside from getting to see what bizarre things famous people do when they're supposedly being themselves, these shows are about watching the people we grew up watching trying to figure out what happens when you're no longer what you were—and finding they have no more idea than the rest of us. I'm not sure why it's comforting that mall queen Tiffany is as confused as I am, but it is. If, like the better-adjusted inmates of these shows, we can view the Formerly years not as the sun setting on our potential, but as a shot at being who we are now, this time with a sense of humor, we're in good shape. Pass the Cheez-Its.

My sense of humor on the subject of no longer being young is getting quite a workout. I remember a work party I went to maybe two years ago. Because magazines tend to be peopled mostly by folks under 30, I was not shocked that most of the music played was completely foreign to me. Naturally, the young assistants and associates all knew and loved the songs the DJ was spinning (although, of course, he was spinning nothing, because one cannot spin an MP3 file). They squealed in unison, shouted the name of the artist, dropped their forks and pulled one another onto the dance floor, swaying in rings of fabulousness, their sky-high heels apparently no hindrance to their perfect music video moves. These girls (or women, as I, too, preferred to be called when I was a girl) were gorgeous, joyful and incredible to watch. I sat back with a few other relative dinosaurs, finished everyone's dessert and enjoyed the show.

I wasn't aware I'd been feeling left out until the DJ cued the inevitable '80s and '90s oldies medley—the set included Cameo or Bel Biv Devoe or Salt-n-Pepa—but perhaps I was. I only knew that my body had muscle memory of moving to this music at some point in history, and was aching to do it again. I grabbed my boss, who is also in her 40s, and we wedged ourselves in among the chicas. Yes, I'd had a few, and some unconscious part of me likely wanted to demonstrate that I had busted quite a move in my day. (That would have been right during the 30 seconds in 1989 when using the expression "bust a move" wasn't patently laughable.) Before I knew it, I was breaking out some of my very best dance steps from the vault where they'd been stored roughly since Bill Clinton was in his first term.

I daresay I was doing OK. A crowd of assistants surrounded me and my boss, and, my audience clapping encouragement, I let loose. Nothing fancy, but if Madonna did it in her "Vogue" video, I felt free to employ and even embellish. Out of the corner of my eye, I noticed a young man (who of course was gay and worked in the art department) mirroring me. He danced his skinny, 24-year-old butt on over and we clicked together, the perfect match, improvising and freaking each other and role-playing, and it was wild. I felt ever so slightly badass.

But just as he was getting all up behind me and pretending to grind, I had a split-second wave of horror: Is he dancing with me because I'm such a good dancer and just buckets of fun? Or is he mocking me, "dancing" with me in quotation marks, like we used to do The Bump or The Hustle with those who came of age in the disco era?

What if I was dancing sincerely, while he was dancing ironically? How potentially humiliating!

As soon as the thought entered my brain, however, it departed, leaving a big *So what?* in its place. Who cares if he was dancing with me because I'm a great partner or a great comedy act? We were both having fun, and being a Formerly means that it doesn't matter if it's at my expense. The days of having ego enough to be potentially humiliated are over, so even if I'm sort of the joke of the dance floor (and I'm not convinced that I wasn't), I'm just happy to be in on the joke. Unlike when I was young, there is no way I'd let what I looked like having fun inhibit me from having fun. If the song's about me—say, something from, I don't know, 1974, or better yet, 1987?—great. If not, but it's got a beat, I can still dance to it!

8

The Comfort vs. Style Smackdown

When shopping for clothes that stylishly bridge the gap between too young and middle-aged frump city, neither of which will work for me, I regularly encounter salespeople who do not understand how narrow and precarious that bridge really is. A misguided or too aggressive nudge from one of them can knock me right off that bridge into the troubled waters below, and I wind up looking terrible.

On the one hand, there's "the helper," who is ever-ready with a suggestion about a style that might "flatter" my "mature" figure or camouflage a "problem area" that I hadn't thought to consider a problem before she brought it up. On the other, there are the outright liars, who say I look good in an outfit better suited to Miley Cyrus. What can be even more humbling is the empathizer, whom I encountered when trying on a cute but unsupportive bra. So much of my left breast spilled out over the top that I could have used a third cup to catch the overage. Handing her back the bra,

I joked about how sometimes our bodies don't cooperate with our sartorial desires. "Oh, I know! It's like, my shoulder blades are so pointy!" she said earnestly. All I could say was, "Yes, well, that can be a real problem," before getting dressed and deciding not to shop at her little boutique again.

Clearly, finding clothes that match my new life, which I'm still getting used to, is not simple. When I look at what other Formerlies on the street are wearing, I mostly see women who fall into one of three categories:

1) Those who are trying too hard to look younger than they are. I'm thinking if your C-section scar is visible over your jeans, they are too low. And those shorts and sweats with writing on the ass tend to draw the eye to the ass—something I'm avoiding these days. I'd like to think my ass speaks for itself.

2) Those who seem to think that they are being punished and so are only permitted to shop at Dress Barn. What nimrod thought that was a good name for a women's clothing store? Barns house farm animals. Women tend not to like being associated with farm animals. Even female farmers, who have valid reasons for associating with farm animals, do not want to shop alongside them. (Pottery Barn, however, is OK. They have nice picture frames.) These women look older than they are, like they are in some kind of hurry to make it to the other side of

Formerly and land squarely in middle age, where they think the world makes more sense. I'm told it doesn't.

3) Those who don't appear to be trying at all. I respect these opt-outers, by the way, but I hope they're choosing to live off the fashion grid in defiance of child exploitation or because they prefer to cultivate their inner selves than because they have nothing but sweats in their closet. My friend Kely is an opt-outer most days a week. She drives a mini-van, wears Uggs and has even worn pjs under her coat to drop her kids off at school, "a veritable trifecta of mom-letting-go offenses," as she puts it. She has decided to believe that she is one of those people, like incognito movie stars and models who would look good wearing a mesh laundry bag, who is so fabulous she can pull it off. It works for the three weeks a month she's not about to have her period. "Then for one unholy week you are just a fat, middle-aged, angry woman sitting in a mini-van," she says.

So what's a woman who has lived through the '80s to do, when all of a sudden she is told that the '80s are "back!" and she has a feeling she's not supposed to partake in the plaid mini-kilt and Doc Martens trend this time around? I still want to look relevant, attractive and in-the-mix, of course, and not as if I shop at Chico's. (Sorry, but COME ON with the giraffe prints and chunky faux African beads! That's where I would go if I wanted to look like a college professor emeritus' poet wife.) Then again, I don't want to go around wearing ironic machine-distressed T-shirts featuring cereal box icons from my childhood. My body's not the same as it was, the way I spend my days is not the same, what I want to project has changed and my tolerance for discomfort has certainly changed, too.

That last one is huge. Formerlies are juggling so much (I won't blah-blah-blah you with the litany of roles women our age are playing and how many balls we need to keep in the air—you're living it). Suffice to say that when you feel as if you're perpetually ten minutes late for your entire life; are carrying a briefcase, a gym bag, groceries and maybe a diorama of an eyeball your child made for science; are hungry; need to pee and feel guilty that you haven't had sex with your partner in a month, the last thing you need is for your bra strap to be digging into your shoulder.

And yet, it's still important to you to look good and to feel attractive, even if, like me, you're partnered and so are not actively seeking to attract anyone you haven't already. This push-pull between comfort and style accounts for a large part of my closet paralysis. I think of it as the Comfort vs. Style Smackdown, and which will win depends on the day. See if you follow:

I can remember in my early 20s weaving my way home from a bar in the snow wearing open-toe heels, a mini-skirt and a motorcycle jacket. I'd known it was going to snow—in fact, it may have been snowing when I left the house—but I had a creed that was no less principled than the postman's: Neither rain nor snow, nor sleet, nor dark of night shall stay this vain, silly girl from wearing something inappropriate for the weather if she thinks she looks good in it.

These days, when I rush by just such a gaggle of 24-year-olds outside a bar in the snow with only their hotness to keep them warm, I'm wearing one of those heinous goose-down vertical sleeping-bag coats, a hat chosen for it's ability to cover my ears (even though it destroys my hair) and shlumpy Uggs that make my feet look like elephants' feet. I look like shit, but you know what? I'm warm. Warm trumps sexy any day.

What I've lost in objective hotness I've gained in common sense and the ability to reason—across the board and in all things, but especially when it comes to my fashion choices. Ronni and I popped into a Steve Madden end-of-summer sale last year, and among the fabulously comfortable *and* hot (Joan Jett studs, anyone?) flat sandals I eventually bought, stood these high-concept, architectural marvels. They were some four inches high, with fringes and patent-leather patches and cutouts in the upper (think open-toe-and-heel boots, like a monokini for your feet). I surely would have tried them on 15 years ago, but not this time. Ronni found them laughable, and if you think of them as shoes, she was correct. But if you think of them as little statuettes for your feet—like wearing an Emmy or an Oscar—they were kind of awesome. I would be proud to have one on my mantel, if my apartment had a mantel. And at one time I would have been proud (albeit sorry by Happy Hour) to have had them on my feet.

When I went to pay for my flats, I was telling Ronni how I can't wear heels anymore. Sometimes, I can do wedges, but even they are tough for a whole day. The saleswoman (maybe 25) looked surprised. "I don't know if shoes have gotten more uncomfortable or if my pain tolerance has gone down, but I'm done done done with heels," I said.

"It has to happen sometime," she responded politely.

"Yes, well, it happened sooner than I thought. Ha-ha." There was an uncomfortable (for me) silence. I waited for her to agree that I was too young to be fated for flats forever. But she didn't. She just smiled blankly, in that way people who believe they will always be young and hot (and able to wear heels all day) will do when looking their future in the (finely lined) face. I didn't bother to correct her.

Thing is, I now realize that when you're a Formerly, you need your feet to function. If you have someplace to be, generally speaking, people are relying on you to arrive (perhaps your children or your business partner). It's not, like, *whatever,* if you show up. Tottering or limping in 20 minutes late because OMG your shoes are just killing you and you couldn't find a cab but OMG they are SO CUTE AND TOTALLY WORTH IT isn't an option. Flat shoes: a small fashion sacrifice to make in exchange for being able to walk.

Still, it is entirely possible to take the whole comfort-is-queen thing too far, and I live in fear of that. A 20-something wearing lounge pants from the Gap and a tank top may look a bit sloppy, but still potentially adorable and sexy. A Formerly, not so much. Witness what can easily take place when comfort is the only consideration in the selection of attire. (I have to warn you: This may be difficult to read, but no one who loves you will have the heart to tell you if you are turning into this woman, so it's a good thing I'm here. She lives within all of us.)

It all starts reasonably enough, with a pair of Merrell fleece-lined clogs, quite possibly both the most comfortable and ugliest shoes ever made. You buy them because you need something to run out to the end of the driveway for the paper in (or in my case, down to the laundry room in your building). It's not a big leap from there to shuttle your kid to a playdate in them, and oh, maybe stop at the FedEx Kinko's on your way home. The next day, you slip them on, get the paper, deal with breakfast and then realize you're late for an appointment and figure you can get away with not changing out of the sweats you threw on this morning . . . just to get your hair highlighted and maybe run to the supermarket. The following day, you decide it's OK to not wear a bra, as long as you keep your hoodie zipped. Oh, look. It has a stain. Big whoop. It's not like you're going to the Oscars . . . And on from there.

Before you know it, you are one of THOSE women. You know, the ones that before you were a Formerly you used to look at and wonder how she became one of THOSE women. Eventually, you realize that you only go places—Starbucks, the mommy group, the mommy group that meets at Starbucks—where you can dress like one of THOSE women. That's when you know you're in trouble. When your clothing dictates your activities, and not the other way around, you have crossed over to the dark side.

I must have blocked it out, but when my girls were small, I was one of THOSE women on the weekends and every minute I wasn't at the office (I worked at a magazine that was housed in the same glittering tower as *Vogue, GQ* and *Glamour;* I pulled it together to go into the office because there is an invisible electric fence that zaps THOSE women as they try to enter the building). I know I was one of THOSE women because before I put them in the InSinkErator there were pictures of me looking like a bean-bag chair. Briefly becoming one of THOSE women post-partum or postdivorce or postapocalypse is understandable, of course. The key, as I now understand it, is to remember to come back.

9

The Big Metabolic Fuck You

f your metabolism had a middle finger, it would be wagging in your face right now. That's how I picture mine: like an embittered, withholding ex, claiming the Indigo Girls CDs you've had since college belonged to him and pettily refusing to acknowledge that you once shared something that was, if not perfect, mutually beneficial for a time. If I didn't know that my metabolism wasn't actually a sentient being (and I do know this, despite the fact that I've been overheard cursing it out), I'd say it was out for revenge, as if I'd publicly questioned its virility or left it for a younger, faster metabolism. I did not. I'm the one who was dumped.

I don't see any other way to interpret its attitude. My body has been a gracious hostess, encasing it for lo these several decades. If I am to blame for anything, it's lavishing upon it a few too many empty calories to work with. Is that really so wrong? The Big Metabolic Fuck You (TBMFU, for short) is how it repays me. Nice. Real nice. Attaway to be a team player.

Of course, I am aware of how fortunate I am that TBMFU is, right now, my biggest health issue. It seems just a wee bit Tori Spelling (who was "only" left $800K in her rich daddy's will) to complain about this when there are those whose bodies are failing to cooperate in much more profound and life-threatening ways. But in the absence of a bigger health crisis to worry about, TBMFU—that seemingly sudden refusal of your body to process what you eat without padding your pooch—can be profoundly unsettling to your average female Formerly, who is, thankfully, still relatively healthy.

I never had a problem with my metabolism before now. The problem was with my head. I was a thin kid, but nonetheless believed I was fat and had an eating disorder in my teens. I have spent the years since unlearning how to be a freak about food and just eat normally, whatever that means in a country where it seems as if everyone's either paying for two seats on the airplane or has hip bones jutting out like wall brackets you could set a bookshelf on. My metabolism bore with me as I figured it out, and my weight had been stable and healthy for many years. Probably because I've always exercised (with varying degrees of compulsion); if I lost myself in a can of chocolate-covered almonds and then ate my way back out, it was nothing that paying a little extra attention for the next few days couldn't even out.

Then I became a Formerly, out came the middle finger and all of a sudden I couldn't zip my pants.

The reason I'm so fixated on TBMFU (aside from the fact
that weight gain and sluggishness are welcome at nobody's
pool party) is that it is the clearest example of the phenomenon that repeats itself over and over again, when it comes
to the physical aspects of life as a Formerly: I now have to
work even harder to remain *in the exact same place.* Ever since
turning 40, when it comes to my weight, my level of fitness,
how effectively I manage my stress, as well as all the little
stretches and supplements I cannot skip if I am to maintain my well-being, if I didn't redouble my efforts, I'd lose
ground fast. Before long, I'd wind up a large, flabby, anxious
and exhausted nervous system covered with sallow, acned
skin, instead of the vital, radiant, attractive if no longer hot
specimen you see before you (or would if you could see
me). It's like I've stepped on one of those moving side-
walks at the airport, except that it's begun to move back-
ward. It was slow at first, but I'm noticing that now I have to
walk briskly, trot and sometimes jog outright simply to not
wind up back at the security area. Never mind making my
flight.

Some examples, as if you don't have your own: A month-
long stint of lifting weights at the gym previously yielded
visible triceps. Now, if I can coax them out, they must somehow distinguish themselves from the adjacent layer of flesh
that apparently has no muscle in it at all, meaning it's un-
tone-upable. And when I was in my 20s, I could at least *pretend* that if I had the motivation to do all the crunches that
the magazines I wrote for advised, I would have flat abs.

Now, after having twins and actually doing those damn crunches (and Pilates and planks and all the other core tighteners), I know I never will. Nothing short of a doctor slicing a big Cheshire cat grin from hip bone to hip bone and lashing my separated stomach muscles together will give me those elusive flat abs. (That's actually how they do it!) And that's not going to happen.

My friend Maryn wasn't a big fan of her metabolism even before TBMFU. When hers slammed on the breaks, "I felt like, oh, great, this is like having a bad relationship with your mother, and then having an argument with her." Maryn earns her living writing about bizarre epidemics like MRSA and swine flu that everyone worries disproportionately about while millions of people do their grocery shopping at the 7-Eleven. Maryn was never thin, but neither was she heavy, and now it's even harder to be, well, not heavy. She likes wine. She likes a good meal. These are not crimes. As a health writer, Maryn knows exactly what she should be eating and how much. "But emotionally I'm in complete revolt against that," she says. "I feel like one of my few routes to uncomplicated pleasure has been taken away by my body's misbehavior."

Maryn swears there was an audible click when her metabolism went into energy saver mode, but for my Formerly Metabolically Blessed friend Karen, the slowdown was more gradual. She was a little slip of a Madonna-loving, bar-hopping, late-sleeping girl when we hung out in our early 20s. "I ate anything and I never thought about it twice. I was on the smoking-waitressing-drinking-till-4:00 AM diet," she says. At the time, she was working and putting herself through school. Now she's got the degree and is married to a lovely guy who likes to cook her romantic 9:00 PM dinners after they both get home from work, and then settle in for an evening of cuddling and watching movies. Her job as a production coordinator for commercials is less physically taxing than was hoisting huge trays over the heads of wild Wall Streeters, and she's also had two kids. How much of any of our Formerly-era weight gain is due to TBMFU and how much is due to the combo of eating more, moving less and losing metabolism-boosting muscle mass is probably pointless to tease out.

Nowadays, Karen probably couldn't wait tables as she did back in the day, not that she'd want to. She's not in fighting shape anymore, but even if she were, she'd have to pay a hefty Formerly Tax for her exertions, because her body's recovery time has slowed down as much as her metabolism. When I'm feeling sunny and at one with the universe, I decide that the fact that I'm disinclined to do the things I did in my 20s—work late, go out and get silly drunk and then arrive home late and have cereal for dinner before sleeping five hours and doing it again—is my body's way, in its infinite wisdom, of protecting itself. Other times, I think it's because I'm a big old slug. Oh, you can still have a good time. But as a Formerly, it'll cost you. To wit, here's how much you'll pay for any fun you have:

The activity: having a few drinks

In your 20s: no consequences

As a Formerly: You will sleep poorly, endure a dull headache and be irritable until you retire early the following night.

The activity: getting rollicking drunk

In your 20s: a possible hangover, but nothing a good puke, going back to bed and then eating a plate of toast and greasy eggs won't cure. Up next: a little hair of the dog that bit you.

As a Formerly: The room will spin until you drift off into the fitful sleep of regret, wondering if you said anything that can ruin your career. The next day you will need to remain in a darkened room and the slightest sounds will send waves of pain through to the arches of your feet. Your spouse will have to mind the children all day, and he'll be pissed because he controlled himself and only had a few drinks (and so has a headache, see above). You will then owe him big, and for that, you may resent him.

The activity: going dancing

In your 20s: no consequences, except, perhaps, blisters

As a Formerly: Your knees will hurt, but mostly your ego will, because you'll realize how hopelessly out-of-date your moves are and that you get winded after two songs instead of being dragged off the floor and poured into a cab as in days gone by.

The activity: playing a quick game of pickup football

In your 20s: a few scrapes or bruises

As a Formerly: It depends with whom you're playing. If it's with children or merciful teenagers, you might have a bit of joint discomfort from quick lateral movements—a few Advil and you're good. If it's with a male Formerly with something to prove, you are in grave danger of dislocating a shoulder, getting your ribs crushed, your muscles pulled and reigniting every sports injury you ever had. You will be in pain for at least two days.

The activity: impromptu roughhousing with children

In your 20s: no consequences

As a Formerly: There is risk for spinal injury, pulled muscle or hernia, depending on the weight of the child or children. Possible flying boogers increase your chance of contracting a cold bug, which will linger longer than it did when your immune system was in tip-top shape. Remember: Playing with an unwashed child means you're playing with every child they've ever played with.

The activity: staying up all night chatting with friends

In your 20s: no consequences

As a Formerly: All-day headache, which leads to over-caffeination, which leads to nausea and agitation and anti-social tendencies. One hundred percent chance of bingeing on carbs the next day, because your judgment is impaired, your mood is for shit and your body is craving extra energy. Overdoing the carbs, of course, leads to overnight weight gain (see TBMFU), plummeting blood sugar and rebound bingeing.

If you forget you're a Formerly and feel the abovementioned effects, you may think you're unwell. This would not be illogical. The conventional health wisdom is, if you're doing what you always have and notice your body reacting in a way that's not normal for you, there might be something medically wrong. If the problem persists, it would be wise to consult your physician.

That's what I did when I started feeling a little funky. Around the same time as TBMFU hit, and around the same time I noticed my energy falling off, I also began to notice that I had a lot less hair (on my head) than I used to, and a lot more hair (on my face) than I used to. I didn't go right to the doctor, but began doing what doctors hate us to do but do all the time themselves: I Googled my symptoms. The condition that kept coming up was hypothyroidism, which is when your thyroid, that little butterfly-shaped gland in your neck, doesn't crank out enough of the two big thyroid hormones. This, in turn, has a cascade effect on a bunch of other hormones and systems in your body and causes you to turn into a man. Well, not really, but the symptoms are unpleasant (unexplained weight gain, fatigue and depression, to name a few) and if left untreated can lead to heart disease, infertility (Hello! Already had that!) and a few other lovely things that no one wants.

When I saw unexplained weight gain and fatigue—

problems I'd reluctantly concluded were the by-products of
not being 25 and of having twins and a full-time job—on
the list of symptoms, hope sprang anew. Hmmm, maybe I
have a sluggish thyroid. It says here it's very common and
underdiagnosed! It says women often get it after childbirth!
And it says it's easily treatable! Yes!!

I practically tap-danced to my GP, who ran some tests and
told me my thyroid was normal. Then I went to my gynecologist and she said the same thing. I asked her if I had a
"subclinical" problem—perhaps, while my thyroid hormone
levels were within normal range, they were at the low end
and hence too low for me. She shook her head sternly. I
couldn't believe it. I didn't want to believe it. I called my
mom. "Mom, the doctors say my thyroid is normal!" I
moaned. "That's great, honey. What a relief!" she said. I almost hung up on her.

The fact that my thyroid was normal was bad news because, in my twisted Formerly way of thinking, it means that
I am not, in fact, slightly off-balance hormonally, but simply
fatter, more sluggish and hairier than I was when I was
younger. WTF kind of diagnosis is that? As sick as it sounds,
at the time, a part of me would have preferred to pay some
huge pharmaceutical company thousands of dollars over
the course of my lifetime through a bloated, mismanaged
health-care system that is burdening the big steaming pile of
dog do that we call the American economy for a synthetic
thyroid hormone replacement (that may ultimately cause
bone loss) rather than accept that my body is changing, that

a certain amount of change is part of life and that the best course of action may simply be to ramp up my efforts to take care of my body so I don't put on too much weight or grow a full beard.

It's like back in my eating disorder days when I used to pray for a tapeworm or be halfway psyched to have a stomach virus because it meant I'd drop a few pounds—it's such a warped mentality, and I'm not sure if I feel comforted or horrified about the fact that many, many Formerlies share this view. One article I read referred to doctors having to wipe away tears from women patients who were so attached to the idea that they had a thyroid problem (and thus a solution for the fat-tired-hairies) that they broke down when pronounced healthy.

My friend Jen M. has many of the same symptoms I have. "I was training for last year's Chicago Marathon, and in the past, anytime that I trained that hard, I lost weight," she says. "This time, I not only didn't lose weight, but I gained some, and I didn't do anything differently." Jen, too, went to several doctors, each of whom confirmed that there was nothing wrong with her thyroid. One had the gall to suggest that—get this!—she was simply getting older. Jen hasn't given up on the thyroid theory just yet. She's taking sea kelp, which is thought by some (and by "some," I mostly mean those who manufacture sea kelp supplements) to help stimulate the thyroid; as of this writing she hasn't noticed a change, and has also been watching what she eats even more closely. "I don't want to believe that it has to do with my age," she says.

(In fairness, it could be that there's no solid scientific evidence behind sea kelp as a thyroid stimulator because there isn't much financial motivation for pharmaceutical companies to fund double-blind, placebo-controlled studies on things like sea kelp, which is abundant and inexpensive and so they can't make much on it. Those gold-standard studies are the best way to know how well a drug or a supplement works. That said, considering how desperate people are for a metabolism fast-forward, somehow I think it would have risen to the top of the market if it was the proverbial magic bullet. Although I hear the Little Mermaid swears by it.)

What makes this particular condition, hypothyroidism, so bizarrely desirable among Formerlies is that it's at the center of the health/vanity nexus (Weight gain! Hair issues! Zits!). It also shines a white-hot spotlight on the question we seem to be deeply ambivalent about finding the answer to: What is simply a normal part of getting older, and what is a disease, or the beginnings of one, that can be treated, thus making your life better while you're living it?

I, for one, am not sure I want to know the answer to that question—am I getting older the way a healthy person generally does, or are my symptoms a sign that something is off, and once I'm better, I'll be back to my old self?

If the answer is, *Sorry sister, suck it up, hair thins as you age and a little weight gain is typical if not healthy, and well, you're Jewish, and women of Mediterranean descent can be furry creatures, especially when their hormones go haywire,* that may just deplete my self-acceptance account for the foreseeable future. It took me all of my 20s and a chunk of my 30s to get over the whole you-have-to-be-perfect bullshit. Don't I get to enjoy myself for a while before I become even less perfect? Do I *really* have to start accepting that no matter how much laser hair removal I have, there will be more hair? I'm so over it.

If, on the other hand, the answer is, *No, you're fine, take a pill, or an herb, or some sea kelp,* then I don't have to deal for a while. That's rather appealing. I remember the rush I felt when I thought maybe—just maybe—all these little thieves of my hotness were merely symptoms of a treatable medical condition. The hope I had, until it was shot down by the doctors I saw who assured me I was healthy, goddamn it, was exhilarating. And that's what keeps us looking for that magic bullet, whether it's a diet pill or a thyroid pill or a tea brewed from a type of bark natives of the South Sea Islands have been using as home insulation for centuries. Even Formerlies who know there's no such thing as a magic bullet still pray to get hit with one.

Since that's not likely to happen, I have one thing to say to my old friend metabolism: You do what you have to do. I respect your choices, even if I don't agree with them. Yes, I'll pay attention to what I eat—I'm plenty vain and health-conscious enough to do that. I'll keep exercising and eating right, within reason, for God's sake. But you know what? If enjoying my life means forgoing the skinny jeans (which didn't look good on me in 1982, the first time they were in style), I think I can live with that. You hear that, metabolism? I'm moving on. And you can keep the Indigo Girls CDs, even though they were MINE in the first place. Someone has to take the high road. Besides, I can download the good songs.

10

Minor Miracle

Predictably, a few years ago, my Formerly husband and I went in for the all-inclusive resort family vacation we thought we'd never take. All of a sudden, the upside of a Kidz Club and a pool with a waterslide outweighed the fact that we had turned into the supremely uncool pair that we swore we'd never be on our honeymoon, when we climbed Mt. Etna with nothing but a couple of water bottles the day before it erupted.

All this to say I had to go swimsuit shopping. The only thing I had in my drawers were bikinis, which were ill-advised before I had twins. I had never had a flat belly, but as a younger woman, I sincerely thought it was a good use of my time and energy to do a zillion ab exercises and, what's more, to consciously try and hold my navel to my spine all day long at the beach or the pool so I could wear a bikini. As a Formerly, I now have way too many things to think about to waste one second mapping out exactly how to rise from a towel without accentuating my belly rolls. What's more, no amount of not breathing or not eating would make my tummy flat. Yes, it was definitely time for a one-piece.

I went to a large department store, figuring on a wide selection. An older, career saleswoman approached and asked if she could help me, and I told her I was open to anything, but no bikinis. She nodded knowingly.

I felt as if she were a flight attendant walking me slowly and cruelly past First Class, through Business, past the comfy bulkhead row, to my nasty seat by the toilet with the broken lock in the back of the plane. She steered me beyond the pretty prints to an area where the suits were mostly brown or black and had words like "miracle" and "tamer" and "molded cups" in their descriptions. She was a "helper." Had I asked for the serious supportwear, that would have been one thing. But I hadn't. It was as if a waiter brought me a Diet Coke, when I'd merely ordered a cola.

I looked back over at the sea of suits we'd passed, told her these "miracles" were a bit much for me and declined her further service. I didn't think my body needed to be *too* tamed or molded, and I was saving any miracles I might have coming for if, God forbid, one of my children got sick.

My remaining choices, however, after eliminating the miracles and the bikinis, hardly made me want to go on a bathing suit buying bonanza. In fact, these paltry options seemed to create more problems than they solved. There were the one-pieces meant for serious lap swimming, with the high necks, boobs smushed down and the racer-backs. Those look brutal on everyone. I tried a few "tankinis,"

which are like the assisted-living facilities you go to before
you need the round-the-clock nursing-home-type care of
the Miraclesuit. The separate top and bottom allow for ease
of peeing—always appreciated—but otherwise it's unclear
why you'd bother. Do the swimsuit manufacturers want to
gradually get us used to the idea that our two-piece days are
ending, and see the tankini as some kind of a step-down system? I suppose by revealing just a sliver of tummy at the bottom, one hopes to create the illusion that the rest of the
abdomen is just as pristine as that one-inch strip, instead of
the pale, stretch-marked, possibly postpartum pile of pooch
that it is.

And of course, there were the backless tankinis—you
know, the ones that are like bikini tops with a flap of fabric
hanging down in front like a doggie door, to cover the belly.
To me, these say nothing so much as "My tummy is atro-
cious, but everything else is passable." Think Groucho Marx
glasses with the big shnoz and moustache attached, except
not for your face but for your torso. No one is fooled by
such a flimsy disguise; for me, anyway, a one-piece felt more
dignified. At least some came in nice prints—mandatory
"slimming" monochrome at my age? I'm pro-choice.

I wound up getting the single, solitary bathing suit in the
entire store that worked: a '50s-inspired one-piece seemingly custom-made for my '50s-style body with its mom-
hips and -boobs (Restraint says homage is okay—it's not the
same thing as irony). I am so *From Here to Eternity.*

The experience, insulting and depressing though it was,

helped me figure something out: I'm not ready for compensatory dressing.

I love that term—Nora Ephron coined it in her book *I Feel Bad About My Neck*—and we've all done it to an extent. She was referring to items such as turtleneck sweaters chosen not because she adores turtlenecks and thinks she looks terrific in them, but because she dislikes the loose skin on her neck and sees it as something of a public service to cover it up.

God knows I relate to the impulse. Like most women, there were chunks and jiggly bits that I would have just as soon shrouded in strategic mesh or lace even when I was younger and closer to the ideal. But now that the entire lower half of my body has been ravaged by childbirth and the flesh of my upper arms has declared independence from the rest of my body, compensatory dressing as a strategy has gained even more appeal.

But the molded-cup lady confirmed for me that I'm not going to go there, at least not now. There are several reasons for this. The first is something of a principled stance—not the loftiest ideal in which to stick my flag, but it's the best I can do for now: This is my body, floppy though it is, and within reasonable limits and standards of obscenity, it is the world's obligation to deal with it.

I don't always carry this "my ass, love it or leave it" attitude in my heart, especially after discovering a new pucker or stretch mark. But after so many years of looking in the mirror and critiquing my reflection, I've decided to act as if, in hopes that I come to believe it all the time. And it's working. As a Formerly, I feel better about my body, even as it gets "objectively" worse. So I'm not buying clothes to hide all the imperfect parts. Not for nothing, I'd have to wear a burka.

The other big reason I'm not doing the compensatory dressing thing is that (Formerly Hot though I am) I have decided that I still look too damn good to choose a swimsuit or any item of clothing primarily for what it hides. If I did, I'd be hiding my light, my mojo, my personality, which would make me feel way older than my newly floppy arms make me feel. So no, the skirts I wear don't have to be microminis, but I'm not going to go all Mormon fundamentalist because my legs have a few new spider veins. The vast majority of Formerlies likewise look much better than they imagine they do, given all the changes they're noticing.

Case in point: I have a very close friend, a Formerly with a lovely, if imperfect, postpartum body, whose favorite bathing suit is a marvel of engineering. There are several overlapping panels of high-tech fibers designed to flatten and smooth her belly and hips. Which they do. Fine, but the rest of the suit looks like something an East German Olympian would have worn back when there was an East Germany (and yes, I've said this to her face—I'd be a rotten friend if I didn't). So in love with the possibility of minimizing her smushy bits is she that she sacrifices too much to do so. If she'd simply put on a pretty maillot, even if it didn't have Super Power tummy control or whatever they call it, people would be looking at her world-class hooters or her long, lovely legs instead of that royal blue, black and red monstrosity with the strategic ruche and funny little skirt attached.

I suppose I *could* wear my old bikini, look blobby in it, feel blobby in it and try not to let it bother me. That would be more consistent with the "my ass, love it or leave it" stance. But I find that being a Formerly is all about moderation and adjusting your principles to work with the reality of your life. There's no inherent upside to wearing a bikini rather than a one-piece if you find your own belly rolls distracting, as I do. Just because Valerie Bertinelli wearing a bikini on the cover of *People* makes it seem like the Holy Grail, it is so not. You don't get some kind of special eulogy or dispensation for entry into heaven at the end of your life for having gone out in public with your midriff showing. You should wear whatever is going to allow you to have the most fun at the beach—and to not pass out from low blood sugar in the months before you go. If this is a Miraclesuit, by all means, buy one! I have no problem with making choices like this, between two equally viable options. But picking between two good options—cap sleeves versus short sleeves, for example—is as far as I go with the compensatory dressing. No long sleeves in summer! Hadassah arms be damned.

11

Vanity and Sanity

L ately, getting to the gym has been a struggle. Used to be, I was pretty good about it—four, five times a week, even when I was feeling a little logy. Especially when I felt a little logy, because I chose to believe what all the women's magazines I write for have said: that working out gives you energy, even as you expend energy climbing endlessly to nowhere on a machine made by someone who must have had a terrible childhood. The theory defies physics, of course, but then, I was applying eye shadow during physics in high school and I needed as many reasons as I could muster to get my fanny on the cardio machine.

I worked out as much as the ~~masochists~~ experts say you should, not because I'm so virtuous or an athlete or find the "scene" at the gym scintillating or enjoy watching middle-aged men do things with weights that are only going to make our health-care crisis worse.

No, I went to the gym for two simple reasons. 1) I was just

vain enough (I look better when I exercise) and 2) just grouchy enough (I'm in a better mood after I've worked out). I knew that if I didn't, I would become someone I can't be around. Which is a problem, considering I'm stuck with myself, and so are my kids and, arguably, my husband. I went to the gym in the same spirit in which I brush my teeth: There is little enjoyment but not doing it wasn't an option, either. I felt gross when I didn't go, and analogous to minty fresh when I did.

Hence my dilemma. I'm becoming a teeny bit less vain as I get older—overall, an excellent development, one that gives me a sense of peace and relief, but one that is nonetheless significantly reducing my desire to exercise. I no longer feel terribly gross when I skip the gym for a day, two or even three. In fact, it feels like the natural order of things—why would I go to the gym, really, when it's not going to make as much of a difference in my appearance as it used to? My second reason for going to the gym is still there (I'm still prone to the grumpy blues) but now that I care a bit less about how I look, the ratio of vain to sad and anxious is off.

Does this mean I need to become *more* emotionally off-balance to compensate for caring *less* about my looks, to ensure I get a healthy amount of exercise?

I hope not, because then I'm just a hop and a skip and a deep global recession away from bag-lady city. For all I know, that woman who wears everything she's ever owned and mutters to herself on the street was a Formerly and a mom

of two who simply lost her vanity, upped her mental insta-
bility, saw her 401(k) go down the crapper and now gets her
exercise by wandering from homeless shelter to homeless
shelter. Some days, the bag-lady image is enough to get me
there. Other days, not so much.

12

Of Two Minds, One Body

Lest I have given you the impression that once I (ding!) finally grasped that the cause of my strange disquietude was that I was no longer hot, at least not in the same way I used to be, I settled smoothly into my new iteration as a Formerly, that's not quite how it happened.

Okay, that's not even remotely how it happened.

It certainly helped me feel less nuts to recognize that I was undergoing a subtle but nonetheless all-encompassing life change that ran much deeper than the crevasses between my eyebrows. But the realization alone hardly made me want to go skipping through a wheat field, arms open wide and ready to embrace my future as an aging woman and all the joy and wisdom and reverence from society to which my new status entitled me.

Nay, it was a herky-jerky, one-step-forward-two-steps-back trippy odyssey fraught with insecurity, hypocrisy (societal), hypocrisy (my own), contradictory messages and conflicting, shifting priorities. And guess what? I'm still not there, wherever "there" turns out to be. One moment, I'm laughing with my children, enjoying my work, hugging my husband or walking down the street on a crisp, clear day just glad to be wise and aware enough to appreciate how lucky I am and the enormity of all that I've built and have been gifted. This understanding of my good fortune has come with age, and the fact that nothing lasts forever only enhances the experience for me. I am as wealthy as I could ever hope to be. And, not coincidentally, I feel beautiful.

Then, later that very same day, I'm examining my tired eyes in that stupid 15× magnification mirror I told you about. The skin underneath is newly adorned with tiny white bumps and dark patches, a blue vein that I'd barely noticed before appears to be throbbing cartoonishly and my skin is sallow and looking subtly more slack. A mild panic mixed with exhaustion sets in. I start to ponder "what can be done" about it all. I completely forget that that same face had only recently been smiling and laughing, and, as some cheesy Hallmark plaque over a receptionist's desk I read once rightly said, "A smile is an instant face-lift." I'm back to looking at my outsides, my brain churning with ways to keep them from revealing that too much has changed with time. Only hours before, I was splashing happily around in all that had changed internally for the better.

It's a little schizo, I know, but it's where I'm at. I am of two minds about the way I look (which, as I've said, is just fine), the way I no longer look and how important it is to me as I get older. I am of two minds, and both of them overthink things. I see no solution save learning to roll with how I feel at any given time. So that's what I'm doing, bumpy though the ride sometimes is.

And bumpy though my body sometimes is! Always is! Not that it was ever perfectly smooth, but with pregnancy and childbirth, creeping weight gain and the general southern migration of all the fleshy bits, it really isn't hanging together quite the way it used to. I've been resisting incorporating "shapewear," which is what they're calling girdles these days, into my regular underwear routine, as many of my Formerly friends have, because I find it uncomfortable. But of course there's that other definition of comfort, as in, *I'd like to feel comfortable wearing that slinky sheath dress, and I don't because I'm too fat/rolly/whatever,* which can be just as powerful a consideration.

Superstrong body squishers like Spanx are the nexus of these two ideas: Can you smush your body into a physical shape that makes you feel *psychologically comfortable* wearing a sexy dress, and still feel *physically comfortable* enough to sit, stand and wriggle out of it when you have to go to the ladies' room? There is shapewear for virtually every part of the body, including one's pelican-beak-like upper arms.

And then there's that third comfort, which is to say, ideologically comfortable with the idea that a woman should have to endure one second of physical discomfort for psychological comfort. Why can't I feel sexy in a sexy dress the way I am, which is admittedly a bit on the loosey-goosey side?

My husband works for a congressman, so last year we were gearing up to go to President Obama's inauguration. There are not many events or many men I'd compress my intestines for, but this President is one of them. I went and got me some Spanx, but my two minds had a good long argument about it.

On the one hand, shapewear (remember Scarlett O'Hara getting her corset stays tightened to bring her waist to 17 inches?) is a godsend to many Formerlies. Part of me thinks, whatever gets you through the day, date, red carpet paparazzi gauntlet or Civil War is fine.

But there's another part of me that resents having to even *think* about wrapping my body in sausage casing in order to feel I look acceptable. I mean, really! I'm a Formerly. I am smarter, cooler, funnier and more comfortable with myself and the world than I've ever been, and yet I am considering tucking my belly rolls into a pair of Power Panties or something called a Slim Cognito, which goes from my knees to my sternum and hooks to my bra so it won't roll down when I exhale? Weirdly, the grumpier I get about the idea of Spanx, the better I feel about being a Formerly. It wouldn't have occurred to me to resent it when I was younger—I was too busy feeling fat.

Like most women who give it any thought, I am torn between wanting to feel like I am OK without binding and just plain wanting to look sleek in a sheath dress. Which is why I broke down and got the damn Spanx, as if anyone would be looking at me at Obama's inauguration. (I didn't go—long, irrelevant story—and so I didn't wear the Spanx. They sit in my drawer awaiting another occasion where I'll think it's more important to look good than to feel good—and one will no doubt soon arise.)

In the end, the "to shapewear or not to shapewear" question comes down to the comfort versus vanity balance—i.e., how much discomfort are you willing to endure in exchange for looking smooth and thinner (because they do work!) on any given day. For me, the deeper into Formerly-dom I go, the more I tend toward comfort and away from dresses that require me to smooth my flab. So I wear a slightly looser dress and still look good and can digest my food.

Given the screwy world we Formerlies must navigate, I'm glad such garments exist, I suppose. The last thing a Formerly should have to be worrying about is her lumpy butt, ever, and if a pair of Spanx gives her a reprieve, then fine. I just wish none of us was worrying about it in the first place, so shapewear would be obsolete.

It's not just my body that I'm of two minds about, either. Lately I've been getting bad face days, maybe twice a week, usually when I haven't had enough sleep. Unlike bad hair days, these are much harder to disguise; there is no headband or gel or baseball hat for a bad face day. There are no Spanx for your face. Sure, there are creams and serums that over time might make a drop of a difference. And there are expensive poisons that doctors might inject here and there like the guy at the automotive body shop might bang out dings and dents, if you have the money and the inclination.

But on any given morning, if you wake up with creases and craters for pores, and dark chocolate croissants under your eyes, and blemishes not next to but *on* your little wrinkles, and broken capillaries—oh, yes, and let us not forget, whiskers, the man kind—you've got no choice but to stare yourself down, go through your ablutions and then start spackling on the concealer if you have vanity enough to do so. Which, God knows, I do.

The good news is, after about 45 minutes of being vertical, many of the symptoms of a bad face day (puffiness, sheet cleavage on your chest, indentations on your cheeks from the chandelier earrings you fell asleep in) subside on their own. Others can be painted over. Still others can be yanked out with tweezers or, yes, shaved if things get really out of hand. Failing all that, there are ginormous sunglasses that hide half your face.

Still, if I said I was loving the way things are trending, my nose would grow and that would make a bad face day much worse. Granted, I'm more immersed in this topic than is probably healthy for me, because I recently covered beauty for a magazine. In some ways, though, being privy to the more extreme thinking in the beauty world snaps me back to reality. As startled as I sometimes am by my own bad face days, I am regularly more horrified by the kinds of stuff that are available to potentially alleviate them. This list is incomplete, but it is absolutely, 100 percent truthful. I have heard about:

- A perfume that I'm told is clinically proven to make men think you are years younger than you are
- A product that treats the scourge of "aging fingernails"
- A foot treatment to help protect against "old feet" (that would be, feet that have been crammed into pointy, uncomfortable shoes for the sake of hotness for far too long)
- A skin serum—launched in time for Thanksgiving— to help you avoid "turkey neck"
- Several lines of anti-aging hair care products (not the expected hair color to hide grays, but shampoos and conditioners designed to make the texture of your hair appear as if you had as much estrogen surging through your blood as you did when you were 16)

And these on top of the usual creams, lotions and potions that have targeted the areas women were already worried about revealing their age, such as their under-eye area, their hands and their décolletage. They make me think about parts of my face and body that hadn't occurred to me that might be broadcasting my age (Attention shoppers: I'M 42!!!!), which is, of course, the point. And then they made me giggle. And then they made me annoyed. Really? My fingernails?

But at least most of these products are not advocating violence. There was an ad for a face product that popped up on the right side of my Facebook page about a year ago that made my arm hair stand up. It said, "Murder Wrinkles."

Murder? Isn't that a little harsh, even for something so un-welcome as a wrinkle? Good people disagree on whether the death penalty is appropriate for exponentially more heinous crimes than making someone (who is, after all, not a teenager) look her age.

I kept an eye out for similar language in other appearance and anti-aging marketing and articles. Here's what else I came across: "destroy" (mostly with regard to fat cells), "blast," "torch," "melt" (fat and calories) and "annihilate" (belly fat, in particular). Do the employers of these words forget that the wrinkles and flab are actually attached to human beings? There's bound to be collateral damage. I'm looking down at my belly rolls right now. I've often wished they'd magically vanish or be sloughed off with a loofah in the shower, but these words make me want to hide them like Anne Frank until the war is over.

The violence in these words reminds me of when I was a teenager and so consumed with self-loathing that I tried to starve my body so it would disappear. When that didn't work, I tried to torture it into thinness by overexercising and throwing up. My body didn't like that too much, not to mention my psyche or my tooth enamel. I won't tell you that my body and I got on the Love Train and rode it hap-pily ever after to the terminus together, but when I gradually dropped the adversarial "me versus it" attitude, "it" became a part of me again, and we began to work together to at least be healthy and try to get along. For the most part, we have.

And here we are, 25 years later, and I'm being told to blast and destroy and murder it? I like myself too much to do that. The thing I've learned in lo these several decades is that as looks-concerned as I remain, there is a soul-sucking element to caring too much, to worrying too much and to giving too much credence to the external, and hard as it is to do some days, it is to be resisted.

The best way I've found to do this is to laugh at myself and the changes that are afoot. Luckily, there's no shortage of material, and my daughters are quite generous in helping me out in this regard. One afternoon last spring, when my husband was out with the girls, I seized the opportunity to do a closet purge. I made a huge pile of warm-weather clothes and determined to designate them fit to put back in circulation, to donate or to be saved for my daughters (maybe they'd eventually think they were cool and retro). I was still sitting amid the heaps when the crew came in, so I got up from my task to go greet them at the door. I grabbed something to put on, a black denim skirt that I wasn't sure fit. I yanked it over my thighs, pausing at an obstruction (my ass) that was a bit of a challenge, but nothing a bunch of hopping up and down couldn't overcome. Finally, I sucked in my belly and wrestled the zipper up. The skirt flattened my butt into nothingness and made my stomach pooch out more than usual, but I was kind of psyched I could zip it. I shuffled to the door.

Sasha ran up and hugged me. "Nice skirt," my husband said. After eight years of marriage he knows to say such things. He was not taught this at the Ivy League college he attended and to which he still sends checks; I had to home-school him.

"Thanks! It fits. Kinda." I hugged Sasha back, her face at the level of my abdomen. She pulled her head back a few inches and head-butted my belly. Her forehead sprang off it like it was a mini-tramp, and she laughed and did it again. "It's springy, isn't it?" I laughed, conscious of demonstrating how supremely comfortable I am with my own body (at that moment, I believe I was), to set a good example for my daughter.

"Yeah," she said, laughing, too. "That skirt makes it look like your vagina is in the back and your tushy is in the front." I glanced in the mirror, and lo and behold, that's just what it looked like. And then, while I was digesting that truism: "I can do that with my Barbie," she said.

The "donate" pile just got a bit bigger. Who says real women can't have bodies like Barbie dolls? Hilarious. I'm so glad my body can be a source of mirth and merriment in our household.

That sounded sarcastic, but I truly am. Having my daughters has been a net positive for my body image. Not only do I have to hand it to my body for lugging them around for almost nine months and delivering them safely to the outside world, but mothering two girls has forced me to walk the love-your-body walk and talk the love-your-body talk even when I'm feeling as big as a mobile home and might otherwise be standing in front of the mirror scrutinizing for more signs of decrepitude. Not only do I want to spare Sasha and

Vivian any body angst I can, I simply don't have infinite time to count spider veins or track new cellulite puckers—not when I am so in demand as the shoe tier, waffle toaster and sunscreen applier. Besides, their questions, still innocent and devoid of judgments (at this age, they think I am a combination of Princess Belle and the sun itself, with a little Miley mixed in for the cool factor), remind me that there is nothing inherently ugly about getting older. In fact, some of it is funny, if you can laugh at it. Laughter, even the rueful kind, is beautiful.

A brief layover in Los Angeles or Miami, of course, will remind you that many Formerlies are not laughing when it comes to the physical changes having kids and edging into their 40s have wrought. There is a tendency for women, when they hit Formerly age, to feel they need to pick a lane: You can accept that your face and body are changing, sigh, shrug your shoulders and focus your attention on learning how to properly grow heirloom tomatoes. Or you can go all out to create the illusion that you are not getting older, get tons of procedures and spend your life in a spin class with some sweaty guy with a headset yelling at you, and then go have steamed kale as your postworkout treat. The first adapts her opinion so she feels good about herself as her appearance changes, and the second makes certain her appearance doesn't change, so she never has any reason to have to adapt.

Between these two lanes is, of course, a wide highway of views, and most Formerlies try to stay somewhere in the middle of the road, balancing the desire to look young and fit with the knowledge that, ultimately, there are more important things to worry about, like improving public education and defeating the Taliban. We may even be thinking about these terribly important things as the dermatologist injects botulism toxin into our foreheads, as if that makes it somehow less vain. Or painful. Or expensive. Which it doesn't. But it may make us look less pooped.

On the subject of procedures and surgery, not surprisingly, I tend to veer drunkenly from one side of this busy freeway to the other. Again, I am of two minds. One day (maybe a day that I've slept enough and that dark spot on my cheek that I developed since having the girls isn't particularly visible) I remember that I am a feminist. I decide that what some women do to themselves is nothing short of barbaric, and am ashamed of myself for fantasizing about getting a "mommy makeover," facial fillers and implants that will remain in landfills long after my body has decomposed. I can even muster sympathy for the celebrities who say they "chose" to have plastic surgery and are grateful to have the choice, when really, in the context of their lives, what choice do they have?

And then, the very next day, maybe after a fight with my husband or a day of staring at my computer without typing a word, my principled stance is circling the bowl. I'll stand in front of the mirror pulling the skin around my cheekbones back to see what my face would be like if I didn't have those parentheses around my mouth, as if looking a little less like a primate would help me feel like a more successful human. Hmmm . . . maybe it is a "personal choice" whether to inject fillers into my face. And what is feminism about, really, if not choices?

And *then* I'll feel a little dirty and sick to my stomach, as if I made a compromise I knew in my heart was a poor one. Because in my heart, that's not what I believe.

There's a huge part of me that wishes plastic surgery would simply scurry back into the closet where it cowered before some celebrities felt it was their civic duty as role models to be honest about what they had done, and their right to have done it unashamed. If people were more embarrassed about admitting that they'd had their bodies cut open or the fat sucked out for no other reason than that they could look better longer, maybe fewer people would do it, and the rest of us wouldn't feel so much pressure to keep up with the Joneses, or rather, the (Courteney) Coxes or the (Demi) Moores or whoever may or may not have had work done. When it became socially unacceptable to use racist terms, fewer people did and the virulent ideas they represented were tamped down. Certainly children, unexposed to such hateful speech, were freer to develop different points of view.

My girls are just six and (in response to a question about why, unlike the lady in the magazine, mommy's boobies are so smushy and droopy) I've already had to explain to them that there's no natural way for someone's breasts to sit up on her clavicles.

But while I want my daughters to feel good about the bodies they come by naturally, the main reason I'd like cosmetic surgery to just go away and leave me alone is that—now that it's not only acceptable but being marketed as a feminist choice—it forces me to confront my own hypocrisy on a daily basis, and that makes me terribly uncomfortable. Demi Moore (who denies she has had anything done, and insists she naturally looks like a 30-year-old at 47) is not my role model, and yet I'd rather look like her as I get older than Sonia Sotomayor. I am a hypocrite, and about something that bothers me much more than making my daughters eat Kashi and then sneaking Apple Jacks after they've gone to bed. That's being a tiny hypocrite. I am a gigantic hypocrite. I despise being a gigantic hypocrite.

I would feel more internally consistent if I were the kind of person who could flat-out reject the supermodel body ideal—to say, *Screw you for making me feel I'm not OK the way I am*—and get on with it. But in case you've missed it, I'm only that person part of the time. When I'm not feeling all righteous, I'm Googling various procedures to figure out how much time off from work I'd theoretically have to take if I had them. I feel as if I have an angel on one shoulder, whispering, "Do the right thing. Set an example for your daughters. Show them what you believe in your heart: that there are many ways to be beautiful, and they needn't involve a cannula or a scalpel." On the other shoulder, there is a little Pamela-Anderson–shaped devil saying, "Oh, fuck it, Steph. You've always hated your belly. You've tried to change your outlook and failed. Just get a damn tummy tuck already."

Oh, and I can spend hours staring at pictures of stars who have had botched surgery and so look way worse than they did before. It's sick, and I truly don't wish them ill, but it makes me feel strangely validated.

My friend Sarah, who had breast reduction surgery for mostly cosmetic reasons (she came on like a wall of boobs before and looks much better now) is thrilled with the results and has not a pang of regret. She thinks I'm being way too hard on myself, and holding myself to standards on this issue that most of the world doesn't adhere to. She's right. But one thing I've learned as a Formerly is that if something preoccupies me to the extent that the "to nip and tuck or not" dilemma does, there's probably a bigger issue behind it.

And that issue is this: The fact that it's no biggie to get a procedure or 20 puts many Formerlies in an untenable spot. We are at the precise age where things start to droop and live in a world where looking like a middle-aged woman looks naturally is considered "letting yourself go." This can be profoundly upsetting and seems relatively easy to fix. At the same time, we are finally old and wise enough to know—emotionally know, not just understand intellectually—that looks are by far not the most important thing in the world. My two minds are at war, and they're leaving the landscape of my brain looking like Baghdad after a night of air raids.

What's more, Formerlies like me are experiencing a mass cognitive dissonance—that is, when you hold two contradictory beliefs at the same time, unless you find a way to reconcile them, they will totally stress you out. Many of the Formerlies I've spoken to know that they shouldn't care as much as they do about their aging faces and bodies, and yet they do. They don't want to be "the kind of person" who gets cosmetic surgery (that is to say, vain enough to go that far, to spend that much, to take a risk with their health by undergoing elective surgery), but they really would like to. To reconcile these conflicting desires, they either decide it's not vain but feminist to get surgery (after all, it's a woman's choice and more attractive women stand a better chance in a man's world), or they decide that a procedure is not as expensive or risky or painful as they thought it was. Or they come to feel that they were wrong all along—looks really *do* matter—and that our children may as well get used to the idea. By the time they're adults, everyone will be having cosmetic surgery. Why fight it?

No matter how you slice it, it's a rotten spot for a Formerly to be in. In the same way that I support the men and women fighting in Iraq even though I'm against the war and don't think we should have taken it on, I don't judge women who act on their desire to get cosmetic surgery. I might easily be one of them, and I know that a Formerly's gotta do what a Formerly's gotta do. If getting your boobs lifted will stop you from thinking about how you hate your boobs, more power to you. But just as I don't think war is a great way to solve conflicts and I wish there weren't fighting troops to support, I also wish we lived in a world where Formerlies felt that there was a happy place for them to exist when nature took its inevitable course. I'm hoping that the older I get the more I will resent the idea that I need to stop the aging process, but I can't predict. I don't know if I have the strength to be the one prune in a sea of plums. Time will tell.

Deep breath. Calm down. Stress, I understand, gives you wrinkles and causes your cells to age more rapidly. Now, we can't have that, can we? Especially because I'm told I look pretty good. For my age.

That qualifier started following me around like a hungry puppy in the last couple of years: "For her age," as in, "Stephanie looks pretty good for her age," and "Demi Moore looks preternaturally, extraordinarily, suspiciously stunning for her age, especially since she claims she didn't have plastic surgery."

Of course I realize that someone who says I look good for my age is trying to be kind, to cut me some slack. "For my age," my skin looks nice. I have a decent figure "for my age" and "for a mother of twins." That's clearly meant to be a compliment, in the "considering what you could look like" kind of way. So when someone tells me that for my age, I'm not half bad, I say a sincere thank-you to reward their intent. But it still smacks of *She runs a pretty good race, considering she has no legs.* How cool would it be to hear that your skin looks nice or that you have a decent figure, period, and let the rest be thought, if it must, instead of spoken?

When you're a kid, "for her age" is usually used in the

positive, like Sasha is tall for her (young) age, or Vivian has a large vocabulary for her (young) age. The problem is, of course, that when you're older, what's meant is, *Her skin is relatively unmarred, for her (old) age.* I'm reacting not to the categorization (which I didn't mind one bit when people thought I was poised or successful for my young age) but with my new category, old, or at least not young, is something I'm still not used to.

Come to think of it, I don't mind "for her age" except when it pertains to my looks. That makes sense—getting older has been an overwhelmingly positive transition, except when it comes to my appearance. If someone were to say that I have great vision for my age (which no one would, because my vision sucks), I'd appreciate it, since it's a biological reality that vision tends to get all wonky as a person ages. But that's not the case when it comes to beauty, unless you believe that only young women can be beautiful, which I emphatically do not. Saying that someone looks good for her age assumes that pretty and young are inextricable. So being pretty "for your age" isn't really pretty. It's another category, to be assessed with different standards. It's as if someone told Michael Phelps that he no longer qualified for the "real" Olympics, but a different, by implication less important, Pothead Olympics for guys who like to party, where they gave out those plastic medals you get in the gumball machine that say "You're Number 1" instead of the gold.

Of course, there are plenty of people, like me, who do not agree that pretty is by definition young. But the very fact that I (and millions of other women who make this same point on blogs like mine) have to stand up and counter that idea means it's a pervasive one. So I propose we shelve this particular qualifier, which is truly backhanded, along with the terms "cougar" and "MILF" (short for "Mother I'd Like to Fuck"), which don't exactly advance intelligent dialogue, either.

Putting "for her age" on the shelf is but one tiny step toward marrying my two minds, the one that is grateful for the opportunity to get older, no matter how I look doing it, and the other that is terrified that looking old will marginalize me in the eyes of others to the point where no one will care what I have to say once they see me. That's my biggest fear about looking older: not that I'll wind up alone or unloved, but that I'll wind up unheard. I guess that's why I'm letting both of these points of view continue to debate loudly inside my head, painful as it is to listen to both sides and live with the perpetual conflict. One of my two minds will win out in the end, and I need to be sure it's the one I can live with for the long haul.

13

Mortally Wounded

'd imagine doctors hate being the people who bust women's bubbles by telling them that they're just plain getting older, and there's no cure for the inevitable passage of time. On the other hand, when there is an identifiable medical issue at hand, doctors are good to have around. I just wish I didn't have so many.

A colleague of mine replied on her BlackBerry to an email I sent her, because, she wrote, her computer was down. "My thumbs can't take much more!" I wrote back that she needn't worry, because according to my thumb doctor, it's a myth that PDA abuse leads to carpal tunnel syndrome.

As I hit "send," it occurred to me: *I have a thumb doctor.* A physician specifically devoted to a single digit on my right hand. He's a neurologist to whom I was referred in the fall, after I wantonly continued to cut out pumpkins for Halloween decorations long after the nerve at the base of my thumb had begun to throb. *Must. Finish. Pumpkins.* Compelled by the same force that used to enable me to pull all-nighters for pleasure or enterprise, I sat there cutting out several hundred goddamned jack-o'-lanterns for a neighborhood Halloween party. I was a wild woman! There was no stopping me. And I paid the price. And now I have a thumb doctor. This is what it's come to.

It makes sense that as you get older, you accumulate more doctors. You've had more time bumbling around on this earth to injure yourself and develop diseases and wear out your organs with all that breathing and secreting, filtering and digesting.

But I don't love the way doctors become increasingly focused on smaller and more obscure parts of the body as you get older, unseen "systems" that apparently govern everything from your moods to how much you perspire to how efficiently your cells process that French cruller you couldn't resist at the morning staff meeting. It makes me fear for the future, because I'm sure I'll need a mucous membrane specialist or to consult the world's foremost expert on disorders of the cuticles.

What kills me about all of this is that, aside from a few dings and oddities, I'm a resoundingly healthy person. And yet, I've added far more doctors to my pit crew in recent years than I have aestheticians, and in case you haven't noticed, I care not a little about my looks.

Think about it: Barring any chronic or catastrophic childhood illnesses or conditions, when you're a kid, you have a pediatrician. Later, as a young adult, assuming you have health insurance, you'll have a general practitioner and a gynecologist. Being nearly blind, I also had an ophthalmologist.

It's when you approach Formerlydom that you start racking up doctors like so many refrigerator magnets. If you can't get pregs in the usual way (like I couldn't), you add a reproductive endocrinologist to your roster. And if, when the RE orders the baseline mammogram before he pumps you full of hormones (standard procedure), they find a scary blobby mass with blood vessels snaking around it (as they did with me), all of a sudden you have a breast surgeon! She biopsies the lump and determines that it's benign (whew!), so you're confirmed to be perfectly healthy, if imbued with a new appreciation of your own mortality, and your grand doctor total is up to at least five, six if you count the radiologist. Naturally all this drama makes you a little anxious and perhaps depressed, so you see a psychopharmacologist, who writes you (OK, me again) prescriptions that might help your mood. That's seven.

You get pregnant (yay!), deliver (woo-hoo!), but then your knees ache from all that exercise you've been doing to lose the baby weight and avoid the eventual need for a cardiologist. Time to see an orthopedist (9), who tells you you shouldn't run so much, and that, yeah, pregnancy can screw with your joints, especially a twin pregnancy, which resulted from—you guessed it—taking fertility drugs.

Exhausted and layering on the pounds like there's some impending famine your body is aware of but you're not, you go for a physical. To rule out anything serious, you're sent to a gastroenterologist (9), a rheumatologist (10) and/or an endocrinologist (11) and find out you do not have any auto-immune diseases or thyroid issues. Best they can tell, you are simply pooped because you have twins and have been working too hard and also maybe having too good a time (which now takes a lot out of you) and your metabolism is flipping you the bird.

So you shrug and drink more coffee and cut out pumpkins for Halloween and try not to eat the candy you bought for the kiddies, who are all dressed as Aurora, aka Sleeping Beauty, the most passive and lamest of all the Disney princesses. Creepy. Ouch—you now have a thumb doctor (12). And an allergist (13) and an ear, nose and throat guy (14), because lately you've been prone to sinus infections. WTF? Oh, Christ, I forgot about the podiatrist who dealt with my fungal toenail (15), which, of course, is still there because a fungal toenail will stay with you longer than any lover ever will. So will the lovely cyst on my back (dermatologist, 16).

I have 16 doctors and counting, and I've never had more than a bad flu. I'm not even including the other practitioners, like physicians' assistants, PTs or complementary medicine specialists, such as acupuncturists.

One could argue that I'm healthy *because* I've seen all these doctors, or that the fact that I have seen all these doctors is a sign that I take good care of myself. The second is true. The first is not. Regardless, I would be thrilled to cap the number of doctors at 20 and call it a life.

Anyone would, I suppose. As much as I try to bury it under the many more pleasant things I have to think about, it's getting harder to escape the fact that the older we get, well, the older we get. And whether it's because we're exposed to more sick-making chemicals the longer we live or because the machine of our bodies starts to wear out, we're just now, as Formerlies, starting to notice—weird!—that a pulled muscle took a week to heal, or there's a strange bump that the doctor thinks merits a second look, or that we have things like acid reflux or gout, which sound like old people problems. Plus, hearing of a contemporary who has cancer, while uncommon and still shocking, is not the freak thing it was in our 20s.

Last winter, I had a routine physical with a new doctor I picked strictly because of her proximity to my house and because she took my insurance. Big mistake. Two days later, on a Saturday, as I was walking my girls home from soccer, I got a call from the emergency room closest to our house, the one at the hospital the new doctor is affiliated with. The ER doctor on the phone advised me to get there immediately; my test revealed that my blood counts were so low as to indicate I was bleeding internally, possibly in my brain (!!!). At that moment, I actually felt good—I'd slept in that morning—and told her so. She urged me to come in. I might collapse at any time. She may have even used the word "stat." I sent my daughters off with my neighbor and got in a cab. They admitted me right away, ahead of a guy who had been shot (only in the arm, but how dramatic, right?).

I won't keep you in suspense: Four hours later, worried husband by my side, the results of the repeat blood test came in and I was confirmed fine. The first test had been compromised by my doctor's office somehow, yielding false readings. In those four hours, I ricocheted between thinking, *How ridiculous, this must be a mistake,* and imagining never being able to kiss my daughters on the top of their heads again, and smell their little-girl scalp smell. The thought, even today, is crushing. This wasn't the narrative I could imagine for my own end-of-life story, being called in off the street one winter's day with bad blood and never going home. In fact, I hadn't given much thought to how I might die, but since then, I've been thinking about it more. I don't dwell on it, but compared to never having thought about it as a young person, the entire subject feels new. I still think it best not to envision it.

It's not only that Formerlies have more actual and pseudo-scares now than we did in years past, such as mammogram findings that wind up being nothing (I've had three so far, and like several Formerlies I know, have binge-shopped while awaiting the results of the biopsies). It's also that, as I've mentioned, I'm starting to perceive time as passing faster than it used to. "One minute, girls," shouted through a closed bathroom door seems to take an hour to pass for them, yet only ten seconds to me, and that's not just because it's the only place I have any privacy in our house. I think it's because one minute is a larger proportion of their lives than it is of mine. I feel as though I'm ceding my time to them, like a senator might to a colleague who has more of a point to make. I can only imagine that this feeling grows stronger as you get older still.

And there's nothing like noticing your parents slowing down to cause you to feel every bit the Formerly. My parents remain young of affect, and vital, with no big health issues. Still, it's becoming increasingly clear that I and my husband are on deck. If your parents are older or less healthy than mine, it's scary to think that before long you will not have them to rely upon, assuming they were reliable in the first place. The role reversal, if they become infirm, is difficult for everyone.

But perhaps less expected and more bizarre for some of us Formerlies when our parents get old and need our care is that we often have to knit back together that separation we made when we left home for the first time—and it just doesn't seem that long ago that we left! Depending on what your relationship was like with your parents growing up, having to be close to them in an intimate, day-to-day way can dredge up adolescent sewage better left in the septic tank of your childhood home. I suppose that's one way of feeling young again.

14

The Replacements

A more optimistic way to feel young again, of course, is to have children of your own to drive crazy for the rest of their lives. I've heard people say that kids keep you young, and that's true in the sense that it's hard to take yourself seriously when you're walking down the street wearing a giant yellow construction-paper duck beak that your kid made for you in art class. (The great thing about being a Formerly is that you're unself-conscious enough to wear a giant yellow construction-paper duck beak that your kid made for you in art class.) But physically, children can kick your ass. I have never felt so old as when chasing after Sasha and Vivian. It seems as soon as I finally sit down on the bench at the playground, one of them needs to be taken to the bathroom. They also take a few years off of me mentally, just keeping up with their sharp little minds, as mine gets more and more blunted. I suppose that's natural. They're meant to replace us, and the urge to reproduce is a gesture toward our own immortality.

Much has been written about the mad dash to bear children when you're a Formerly, or at least to decide whether
or not to bear children before the decision is made for you
by your body, which has been preprogrammed to start strik-
ing the reproductive set around age 40. I had my ladies when
I was 35, through IVF. My inability to get pregnant without
help had nothing to do with my age; I had plenty of eggs,
but none of them seemed to want to drop out of the
nest. Still, because I went the high-tech route, and because I
have several single Formerly friends grappling with the get-
pregnant-or-not dilemma who may need help, I've stayed
attuned to what the world has to say about Formerlies having babies.

With the array of stigma-free options for single prospec-
tive moms who want to experience pregnancy and have a
biological child—using a sperm donor, co-parenting with
someone who you're not romantically involved with, egg-
freezing, flying to India for lower-cost fertility treatments
and others—you'd think there'd be this thrill in the air that
for many women, babies that would not have been possible
only a few years ago can now come into being.

And yet, it seems like women are more anxious, not less.
If you're at the choose-or-lose age, you're not only making
a tough decision to deliberately have a baby on your own,
which, while increasingly common, is not easy, you're
making the decision all by yourself—and against your will,
because your hand, or your ovaries, is being forced. Add in
all the judgments that some women place on themselves

about the "right" way to feel in any given situation, and you've got stress with a side order of stress. Instead of covering the fabulous choices Formerlies have arrayed before them, many media treat the to-breed-or-not decision like the alleged mommy wars (aka, some guy's catfight fantasy, recast with MILFs), with all the hyperbole and hysteria that no social or personal issue that men face is ever treated with. Granted, it's a heavy decision, but there's a whole lot more nuance than what you see in these facile takes:

- Women with advanced degrees who have embraced difficult truths in their years nonetheless scaling the corporate ladder, in blithe denial of the fact that their fertility is, in fact, finite

- Women so control-freaky about their fertility that they seek counseling in advance of trying the old-fashioned way for any length of time

- Women wringing their hands, wondering if there's something horribly wrong with them for not really wanting children

- Women pissed that others seem to think there's something horribly wrong with them for not wanting children

- Women wondering if there's something horribly wrong with them for not being "feminist enough" to have kids sans partner

• Women wondering if they've married the first loser with a willing penis in order to get pregnant by the deadline

• Formerlies playing Russian roulette with birth control, half-hoping to get pregnant "accidentally" so they can call their single momhood fate

I'm sure I'm missing some, but do you see a pattern here? Panic, fear, uncertainty, self-doubt and a lot of unhappy Formerlies feeling . . . if not cornered, then disempowered. It's a similar feeling, I'd imagine, to what women who had no option but to marry young and breed dozens of farmhands to till the field must have felt if the biological realities of their lives didn't fit in with their hopes, dreams and plans. And I think that plain stinks.

Look, I know I'd have been profoundly sad if I couldn't have had my girls, and I was fortunate to have a partner at the right time, so I didn't grapple with any potential societal disapproval for my decision, although that's not the kind of thing that tends to trip me up. I remember being initially disappointed that I needed help getting pregnant, and then glad to have science on my side, and the means to pay for it. The fact that many Formerlies have similar options makes it marginally easier to have a deadline on such a huge decision, one that isn't entirely within your control.

But here's the thing: The deadline by which to have a baby—whether you're single or partnered when it hits, and whether that deadline is at age 35, 40 or 50—is still a deadline. As in, you feel as if you will *die* if it doesn't happen.

Of course, you will not die, but you will feel about as powerless as the baby you are thinking of having, only without someone as together as you to coddle you. Formerlies hate to feel powerless. Well, the odd masochist likes it, but only in strictly proscribed situations involving whips and handcuffs. Formerlies in particular, who have just recently come to a place of maximal self-determination, might not be ready to hand over the future of their domestic life to biology and fate (even though these have been largely in the hands of biology and fate this whole time). When you're up against a deadline like this one, it hits you that your choices are no longer unrolling infinitely like the red carpet before you. You already knew this, of course, but now that knowledge has spread down from your brain into your heart and, worse, into your reproductive organs.

This deadline, while set by your body, is entirely impersonal and outside of your control. Where you are in your life simply does not factor in. Which means even though a Formerly has long since gained the wisdom to participate in her own future, she does not get a say in the matter, as if she were a three-year-old being forced into an uncomfortable snowsuit she knows she'll just be sweating in. If this is you, all you can do is protest, ruminate on your options, strategize and feel paralyzed. There simply aren't that many important choices we must make as adults that we truly won't get a second chance on.

The Formerlies who come out of this whole stink pile feeling good seem to be the ones who modify their vision of what their future is going to look like, and use their Formerly wisdom to rethink their past. Instead of deciding they missed their chance to get pregnant the "right" or easier way, they recognize that had the deadline been earlier, having a baby would have been hard for other reasons. If the biological cutoff had been in your 20s, you likely wouldn't have been ready and it would have been an equally tough decision. Likely you weren't equipped in your early 30s, either, because if you had been, you'd probably have a child by now. So here you are, the deadline has arrived, and the time might not be perfect to have a baby under the ideal circumstances. That's nothing new, except that you've used up your deferments.

If, like me, you like to be in charge of your life (I don't mind jury duty; I mind having to go when they say I have to), it's infuriating! But it's not that much different from being stymied by the fact that you weren't born rich or Swedish or with the perfect parents or as one of the Kardashian sisters. You notice, you mourn your perceived loss (everything should have gone according to schedule, but it did not), and then you figure out how to be reasonably happy with the options you do have. Railing against this deadline for too terribly long doesn't bring you closer to a decision, a baby, or feeling happy in your Formerlydom.

It's actually kind of cool, looking back from the other side of the angst, once some kind of decision (any kind) has been made. I have one single friend who had a baby via donor sperm. It wasn't ideal—she had to move back in with her parents for the extra childcare and to save money, but that won't be forever. My friend Sarah is divorced and doesn't want to have a baby without a partner. Since she doesn't foresee meeting someone and building a relationship with him in time to have a baby biologically, she's had to let that go, and will weigh the adoption option if and when the time comes. That wasn't her perfect vision, either, and it was tough rethinking things, but she is happy. I have another friend who adopted from Ethiopia, another who is co-parenting with a guy friend and another who had a baby under the wire with her 10-years-younger boyfriend. She's thrilled about the baby, but the disparity in their ages definitely poses some challenges. That's not perfect, either.

In short, *none* of these scenarios is ideal, but if a Formerly has learned anything over time, it's that few things are—even when you think they will be, even when they appear that way from the outside and even when you do everything "right" and on time. Alas, you can't have everything, and whoever told women we could was an asshole. An asshole who probably thought she was being "empowering," but an asshole nonetheless.

15

Shoe Shopping
and the Denial of Death

My personal stylist, Restraint, who has firm guide-
lines about what I wear, is much more promiscu-
ous with her views on fashion footwear. She has
no issues with my going to town with the shoes, especially
regarding their quantity and degree of flamboyance. I appreciate this about her, even if my husband does not. A few
weeks ago he was nearly concussed by a (gold metallic Sven)
clog when he tried to take something off the top shelf of my
closet (he'll only do *that* once). I gave him the Boo Boo
Buddy we keep in the freezer for the girls, and he didn't say
a word.

What could he say, really? That I had too many shoes? This
is not news, nor is it particularly shocking—many, many
women do, since we love that our shoes still more or less fit
us even if other clothes, over time, do not. He also probably
didn't want to hear me rationalize my vast collection (over
100 pairs), especially because I do it by bastardizing the theory of the renowned cultural anthropologist Ernest Becker,

who wrote the Pulitzer Prize–winning book *The Denial of Death*.

(Bear with me here. If you do, you will be rewarded with an excellent excuse to go out and buy more shoes you don't need and not feel bad about it.)

Inherent in becoming a Formerly is that nagging awareness that you're getting older (not old, mind you, but oldER). It's dawning on you that you are closer to death, whenever it has a mind to pound on your door. In fact, this always has been true, even when you had huge hair and danced with moronic frat boys to Sheila E. in the late '80s. Oh, wait. That was me. Yeah, but I think I saw you there, too, by the keg. And your hair was not exactly small, either.

This was the big idea in Becker's book: He argued that everything we humans do, short of eating and reproducing, is an attempt to defend ourselves against the knowledge of our own mortality. We keep ourselves all kinds of busy studying, working and fighting wars with people who don't believe what we do, essentially to distract us from freaking out about the inevitable. Some of us attempt grand and heroic feats while we're still alive, and thus, symbolically at least, expand our power and live forever. Making a ton of money is one of the big ways some of us capitalists like to think we're going to live forever, at least symbolically.

(Still with me? Just think: shoes, shoes . . . supercute shoes.)

I do not have a lot of money, but I have a lot of shoes. Shoe shopping is the main thing I do to deny death—which,

I would argue to my husband, who daily reminds me that we are On A Budget, is a much less odious manifestation of this phenomenon than starting wars and killing people who don't agree with me, and safer than jumping out of airplanes to prove that I'm not old. It's like, *Take that, death! I have more shoes than I could ever wear out, thus ensuring that they will continue on the journey long after you retire my mortal coil.* And there's nothing like a pair of platform clogs to make you feel closer to God.

Still, it kind of sucks sometimes to not have quite the fashion freedom I had before I was a Formerly. If I wore some funkified getup one day just because I felt like it, people thought, *Ah, youth,* not *Crazy bag lady* or, arguably worse, *Midlife crisis.* I figure, if I can express myself with a wild or at least diverse collection of shoes, what's the harm? I find it's a great way to add a bit of fun to an outfit—ooh, orange suede!—without totally going off the rails on the crazy train. It would be very hard to get up and out of bed and do all the stupid things I have to do each day (like rinse the recycling and go sit in a cubicle and unsubscribe from email lists and find the other pink plate so my daughters quit arguing over the only one I can locate) if I were sitting there pondering my own mortality and how none of it really matters, anyway, right?

16

Circling Vultures

For years I've been watching those Heritage ads, the ones that urge you to buy insurance to pay for your "final expenses," so your family doesn't get left holding the urn. They begin, "If you were born between 1899 and 1950, you are eligible . . ." or some such.

Tonight I was, as usual, listening to Chris Matthews rudely interrupt his female guests, when the commercial comes on: "If you were born between the years 1925 and 1968, you are eligible . . ." Nineteen sixty-eight? Wait a sec, I was born in 1967! The screen then goes blue and flashes the years of eligibility in large, distinct white letters (because if you are between the ages of 40 and 85, you probably can't hear the TV, and your eyesight is no doubt headed south, along with your boobs).

In the space of 11 seconds, the ad made me angry, depressed and then cynical: Being included in the ad's target demographic is classic sales strategy—the younger they hook you, the more money they make. It's kind of like the way tobacco companies used to market to children—if they got you as a teenager, they had you for life. I'll bet the Heritage people and the tobacco people would really hit it off at a mixer.

Then I swung back to being angry. Along with all the responsibilities Formerlies shoulder, with all the stress I have, I'm supposed to worry—right now—about helping my kids pay for the disposal of my corporal remains? They're six; I can't rely on them to dispose of their grilled cheese crusts in the kitchen garbage.

I have a will; we got it after we had children. But to so specifically plan for your own interment? Maybe, *maybe,* when I'm 65. Maybe. Life expectancy for women in this country is around 81. Odds are you've got almost as long as you've been alive again ahead of you to weigh the benefits of cremation versus having your head cryogenically frozen. Sorry, it's not time yet. I resent that anyone thinks people my age consider their longevity that tenuous.

Right now, women are spending their extra money (if they have any after their daughters' passion for American Girl dolls has been satisfied) on Juvéderm, infertility treatments and Spanx. Men are dropping their wads on flashy two-seater cars, $4,000 prostitutes and Wii Fits. Okay, that's mean—some of them are spending them on American Girl dolls, and big diamonds for their wives to show their appreciation for the stress of all those infertility treatments. Many people my age have yet to start saving for retirement, let alone decide between mahogany or plain old plywood.

I don't know about you, but I've got a lot of living to do, even if it takes more than it used to in order to keep myself healthy and feeling good. And if, God forbid, I get hit by a bus on the way to Yogalates tomorrow, I hereby give my daughters and husband permission to cremate me, stick me in a shoe box and drop me down the garbage chute, like we did with the mouse we caught in the kitchen. I fully support their spending their money on pink sparkly shoes for their American Girl dolls and $4,000 prostitutes, just as they did when I was alive. Obviously, I'm not planning on dying any time soon. My new old body, with its brigade of doctors waiting to charge, and its newly noisy quirks and embarrassing leaks, works fine, for the most part.

I'm even getting over The Big Metabolic Fuck You, and am somewhat relieved that hard-core self-improvement is pretty much off the table. My new mandate—that I might gently strive to stem the tide of my inevitable decrepitude, rather than staying on the thinner/buffer/faster path toward some arbitrary standard of perfection that I'd followed all these years—feels like something I can live with, and live with peacefully, now that I'm a Formerly. There was a time when I felt like nothing more than the composite of other people's opinions of me. Now I'm more aware of my value than I've ever been. Sure, one could always be thinner, buffer and get there faster, and I'm no exception, but my as-is is good to go, thank you! I'm just about done with the idea that personal fulfillment is always five more laps, five more lunges, five more pounds away. Physical self-improvement, the drumbeat I marched to in my teens, 20s and 30s, is no longer banging away quite so loudly in the background. For me, that was a losing proposition from the start, and it took me this long to realize it.

As often happens when the rare epiphany shines through the chaos of everyday life, all of a sudden I was tripping over evidence supporting my new way of looking at things. One night at a party, I was chatting with a therapist who treats women with food issues. I wondered aloud if some lucky ducks were simply spared TBMFU. She thought not, that it happens to the best of us, and said that in her experience, Formerly-aged women who are as thin as they were when they were in their 20s are generally very restrictive with their eating. "Apparently it's worth it to them to not eat much," she said with a shrug.

It was an offhanded comment made at a party, and a self-evident one at that. But to me, at that moment it struck me as genius in its simplicity. I could not recall, in decades of wanting to be thinner, ever once asking myself if it was worth the sacrifices it would entail in order for me to actually *be* thinner. The answer may well have been yes when I was younger, but now that I was an adult—a Formerly, no less—with much to think about aside from how many calories were in a single Twizzlers, I wasn't so sure. It takes effort to not eat when you're hungry, to constantly be figuring what you can and cannot put in your mouth based on whether or not you think it'll make you fat or what you may or may not want to eat later. Doing so takes up buckets of mental energy, which can be in short supply when you're already overextended, stressed out and multitasking.

So I asked myself, *Self, is it worth it to completely forgo pretty much all the foodstuffs that bring you enormous joy, such as Nutella and pasta with pesto, in order to be thinner? Moreover, is it worth the thinking and tabulating and calculating and suffering through the guilty feelings you'll experience if you are unable to eat the way you truly must in order to be thin, now that you're a Formerly?*

The answer was a big fat NO. Ha! No, it's not. It's really not.

Before that therapist made her comment, I'd simply viewed my inability to be at a lower weight than what's natural for me as my failing. Now I see it as something not worth expending my limited resources on.

Call it a gigantic cop-out, and I won't argue with you. But that perspective—I've made a reasoned decision not to invest in being as thin as I can possibly be because the trade-off isn't worth it to me—has made me feel better about doing exactly the same thing I have been doing for years: specifically, eating Nutella and pasta with pesto (in reasonable quantities) and feeling like a big loser of a woman without a will. Now I'm eating Nutella and pasta with pesto (in reasonable quantities) and feeling fine about it.*

I'm not going to be truly thin, as in high school yearbook

---

* I specify reasonable quantities for two reasons. For one, overdoing will obviously make you as big as a house, but also because I don't believe there is a permissible quantity of such foods for someone who wants to be high school yearbook thin as a post-TBMFU Formerly. A couple of spoonfuls of Ben & Jerry's and she'd have to fast for half a day. There's nothing reasonable about that.

thin, but I wasn't anyway; desire is not enough to make it so—decades of wanting it really bad and yet not doing what it takes have certainly proved that—and besides, I was bulimic in high school. That was not good. If I'm going to eat what I want and be a few pounds more than I've arbitrarily decided I should be anyway, I may as well feel OK about it.

Lest you think I'm saying to hell with it, your being-fit-and-healthy days are over so you may as well position your open mouth under the soft-serve machine and pull the lever, I'm not. I'm just saying I've found it helpful to quit kidding myself. Yes, my metabolism let me down when I hit Formerly. But more to the point, my life changed, so it's OK if my expectations change, too. The things you used to do to keep your metabolism firing on all cylinders may simply not be as appealing to you as they used to be. And that's fine! You might just not *feel* like running around like a lunatic every night, and stacking your dates (work late, drinks, dinner, club) like you did when you were younger. That used to be fun; it's not anymore. If you've got a partner, you're no longer burning the calories it takes to forage for a partner. There's too much relaxing and clinking of glasses to be done with friends or family in one soft cushy spot now that we're Formerlies. So you're 10 pounds heavier. Find some other way to exercise, eat reasonably and enjoy your life.

17

Having a Fit

One morning, as I stood in front of the closet in my undies, obsessing about what to wear, and my children got later and later for school, something dawned on me. I am not sure why this critical truth took so many years to sink into my thick skull. (Perhaps it was all the fabulous hair I used to have. Did I mention I'm losing my hair?) Still, I'm so glad to finally be possessed of this knowledge and simply must share it with you, just in case you haven't heard the gospel. Here it is. Are you ready? Sit down. This is big.

It is the clothes' job to fit you. It is not your job to fit the clothes.

What's more, this has always been so, and no one saw fit to tell me, even as I spent a disproportionate amount of my mental capital trying to figure out how to make myself smaller. Yes, of course I was aware that clothes came in various sizes, which implied that some variation in body size was acceptable, normative, even. Yet like many young women, I operated under the mistaken belief that I had a designated numerical size, which was usually around two sizes smaller than my actual body, and it was my full-time job to try to make my body fit into "my" size. You don't even want to know what I did to try to achieve this goal.

And all the while, I could have simply bought bigger clothes. Sure, OK, I wouldn't look as thin in bigger clothes as I would if I were, in fact, "my" fantasy size that I never really am, anyway. But since I am *a* size, and I can't go around naked, don't I get to wear the nicest clothes I can find that fit my actual body?

The answer, of course, is yes, now that I'm a Formerly and not laboring under this truly cruel misconception. I no longer buy clothes that I hope or plan to one day fit into. The day is today. The time is now. I have been thin and unhappy, and heavier and happy. I have proven to myself time and again that one thing has little to do with the other, despite all the "I lost weight and now my husband loves me and my life is perfect" ads you see to sell you diet products. I'm wearing clothes that fit, damn it. And it feels, well, like I can breathe again.

18

Married, with Attitude

am pro sex. That's my official stance, and since I started having it in my teens, I have never wavered. I think sex, when everyone involved is happy to be involved, is one of the delightful perks of being human. In theory, I enjoy it very much.

In practice, things are a bit more complicated. Not only must I be relaxed, well fed, but not bloated, and not pissy with my husband about one of the half-dozen petty misunderstandings that take place in a day, but the children must be in deep REM sleep, there must be no laundry, bills or naked Barbies on the bed on which I am to have sex and all computers, cell phones and pagers must be turned off and stowed properly. I'd prefer not to be within a week of the start of my period, be on deadline or feel fat, although I can work around these. The national terror threat-level alert must be yellow or below. Oh, and I also have to be awake, which, after work and kids and everything else, is unlikely after 10:00 PM. And this doesn't take into account whether

Mad Men is on TV, or any of my husband's possible impediments, which, thankfully, are many fewer than mine or we'd never do it at all.

When it does happen, I invariably catch my breath, look over at Paul and say something like, "That was awesome! We should do it more often."

Libido-snuffing lifestyle notwithstanding, I do indeed like sex, even as I have less and less time and energy for it. Years of repetition have made me pretty darn adept and, even with my brand-new body image issues, more comfortable asking for or, failing that, simply taking what I want in bed. By this time, I'm less concerned with whether I'm doing it "right"—there is no right—and what the guy (in my case, my husband) is "secretly" thinking (which, given the relative rarity of the event, is probably *FINALLY!*).

The best part about sex nowadays is that the whole endeavor feels less performative than it did when I was younger, before I fully understood that nothing was expected of me other than to absorb and reciprocate pleasure. When I was in my 20s, I was ultra-conscious of how I presented during sex, like I was playacting some movie-influenced role of "sexy partner," which left me focused on how I was perceived, instead of how I felt. Feeling your way through sex, of course, leads to much better sex for you and your partner. I'm also much less worried about impugning Paul's skill by pitching in in a hands-on way if the situation calls for it. As my friend Keisha puts it, "If I need to, I go ahead and open my own fortune cookie."

Of course, in order to be in the position to have your fortune cookie opened by you or anyone else, you have to have ordered in, and kids are a huge obstacle to even looking at the menu. Even at their most adorable and rewarding, they *will* suck the life out of you during the day. And at night, there's nothing like a groggy child wandering in for some water or complaining of an octopus under her bed just when things might be getting off the ground.

Somehow, making sure our sex life doesn't dwindle to nothing feels like one of my many responsibilities, on par with making sure the car payments are up-to-date, and replenishing the paper towel supply. I sometimes think, *I simply need to make it a priority.* In countless magazine articles over the years, I've quoted dozens of experts about the importance of putting your sex life first.

It's not terrible advice, but I have never been quite able to take it myself. When I consciously think of sex as something I need to better apply myself to, as if I were back in junior high French, I feel overwhelmed and remiss, which further grinds any smoldering spark into the pavement like a spent cigarette. Sex needs to be a priority. Absolutely. But, well, what isn't a priority, really? My children are usually my first priority, along with work, so said children may eat and wear bejeweled Sketchers high-tops, and because I love it. I need to see my friends every so often, and then there's exercise, sleep and "me" time, which are essential to my health and sanity, without which the entire house of cards scatters to the wind. And then there are the countless other things my husband and I like to do together, which feel important for our relationship and knit us together in intimacy—such as, you know, having the occasional conversation. Sex is a priority, yes, but a priority among many priorities I must juggle, which often means it has to get in line. How many things can be critical at once without your head exploding or something falling by the wayside? So I try to fit it in where it fits, without taking it on as yet another obligation, one that I will no doubt fail to deliver on from time to time. Guilt is about the least sexy thing I can think of, aside from leprosy.

I'm told that as kids get older, sex starts to feel less like something that needs to be wedged in between wash cycles, and so becomes more a natural part of life again. I'm counting on it. Of course, depending on when and if you had children, a Formerly's sex life might be just roaring. "We've been at it like bunnies," my friend Danielle, whose husband just had a vasectomy and whose children are in school, confided (and here I am blabbing it!). "Once the kids are a little older, and you don't always feel like, Put your own fucking socks on, things really lighten up and you can enjoy your spouse again. The more the kids can do for themselves, the more you can start thinking about yourself as a person. If you can look at yourself as a person, you can actually give something to your spouse." I can see flickers of a sexier future on the horizon.

My informal survey would seem to indicate that Formerlies, including moms, generally like sex, in theory if not in practice, and that's why I just have to say that terms like

"MILF" and "cougar" really wind my watch. That women who are no longer 21 and also might be parents enjoy sex should not be headline news, but somehow, the world seems perpetually shocked at the concept. That whole Madonna/whore thing dies hard (the Freudian paradigm, not the singer).

Come to think of it, the term "MILF" grosses me out. "MILF" sounds like milk, which, in the context of motherhood, makes me think of breast-feeding. That reminds me of when I had swollen, leaky boobs and sore nipples and had to tote a heavy, noisy breast pump to the office after sleeping a total of four hours at night. The last thought on my mind during the nursing era was of doing it with anybody—least of all a guy who would use the term "MILF." I picture some loser at the beach clutching a beer cozy and rating moms as they walk by his lawn chair on the way to taking their toddler to the potty.

I know of many a Formerly who doesn't share my point of view on "MILF," preferring to accept the deeply embedded compliment that they are still desirable, or at least conceived of in a sexual context. I get that. I usually take the unsolicited thumbs-up where I find it, now that I find it way less than I used to. Still, I can't get past the idea that the very use of "MILF" implies that attractive mothers are such a freaky fringe concept that it requires a separate acronym.

A married friend of mine said she felt complimented when some young guys in a bar she ducked into to pee called her a cougar. But to me, "cougar" (growwwlll!) is even

ickier, connoting a sexually rapacious, insatiable, practically
pedophilic older woman, thrusting her unwanted attentions
and enormous Wonderbra'd bosoms on wide-eyed young
men, or trawling for gigolos on the beaches of Kenya on sex
safaris with her like-libidoed girlfriends. I don't know any
women of any age who "prowl" for sex, and while some
surely exist, they're a tiny, bored minority who probably
don't have a decent sex-toy shop nearby.

For the single Formerlies I know, it's more like, interested
in finding someone to hook up with, yes. She might make
an effort to go out, hopeful of meeting someone desirable
who finds her likewise so they can act on their mutual at-
traction. If he (or she) happens to be younger than she is,
that won't necessarily disqualify him, especially if he looks
like he may know what he's doing. But *prowl* for sex? Who
has time? Who has energy? Please. The word "cougar" signi-
fies that a not-young woman who might actually want to
have sex is so uncivilized that she belongs in a National Ge-
ographic wildlife documentary instead of on a bar stool near
you.

To my knowledge, I've never been called a MILF. This
could be because no one other than my husband wants to
fuck me. I have considered that. But given that men aren't
particularly particular, I'm thinking it's because those I come
into contact with are too polite to use a term like that, at
least within my hearing. And for that, I'm grateful.

I do, however, appreciate when some random person finds
me attractive, as does my friend Amy (agrees with me, that is;

although I'd like to think she finds me cute). Still, there's something palpably different about the experience now that she's been with her husband 12 years. "About twice a year I become dimly aware that some guy is almost hitting on me," Amy told me a while back. "Once the shock and surprise and surrealness wears off, I get a faint wash of gratefulness, drowned out by a motherly, Awww, isn't that sweet." When it happens to me—maybe six times a year, but who's counting?—I feel jazzed, and am comforted that my market value hasn't plummeted too low. I'm not thinking of selling—I'm happy where I am and my marriage has lots of potential for expansion—but I'm not dead, either.

To be sure, that external affirmation from men, which I used to take for granted like the air I breathed, comes my way less frequently. Fortunately, I've learned that unlike the air I breathe, I can live without it, and it means much less to me now that I am solid in that which I offer the world and my husband and others I love. Like sugar, which is horrifically difficult to cut back on but which I've mostly succeeded at, I don't need it like I used to.

Though, like sugar, there is no perfect substitute. In the elevator at my office the other morning, this young messenger was staring at me. Our building is old and the elevator slow. His gaze was lingering, his grin rather . . . sly. *He couldn't be . . . nah. Looking at me? Weird,* I thought. Wait, a full-on smile, with teeth and everything. I thought I saw his eyes dart down to my chest. He *was* checking me out! I pressed the button for my floor and he moved beside me, looking again at my chest. I was wearing a coat, so it didn't feel too sleazy. W*ow. I guess I still have it, at least a little,* I thought, as the elevator lifted off. Check me the eff out! As I strode off the elevator, I felt caffeinated by my harmless ego boost, and took a private pride in my own still-hotness.

Then I got to my office and hung up my coat. There on the right boob area was the neon green adhesive foam "M" that Sasha stuck on me this morning as I was leaving her classroom. "M" for mommy. "M" for moron. "M" for *My God, woman, did you think to look in the MIRROR?* Something else I don't do as often as I used to.

I met my husband, as I mentioned, on the subway when I was in my mid-20s; proof, if all my photo albums were to be destroyed in a fire, that I was at one time hot. I was, you'll recall, "I meet men on the train" hot. And he was adorable— ruddy-cheeked, with curly auburn hair, smiling brown eyes and a naturally broad, buff, athletic body.

Fifteen-plus years later, he's standing in front of the mirror in our bedroom in his boxer briefs and dress socks, flexing his biceps and asking me, "How're my guns?" That's the male Formerly's version of *What if this part here were just, like, up here?* I am on the bed, braless and unshowered, the moustache bleach on my upper lip preventing me from answering. "Yrrr guns looooo gggrrraay, huunnyy," I manage to eke out through my teeth as I pantomime a Mr. Universe pose and throw him the thumbs-up. In fact, they do, to me. Then he gets into bed, I rinse my lip, we watch Keith Olbermann, and fall asleep, exhausted from the day and the kids and Keith's spitting vitriol, and from just being us.

A younger, unmarried person might see the above scene

as an illustration of what a slog marriage is, or as evidence of the oft-repeated point that the spark fizzles once you've been together awhile. For sure, what I just described is hardly going to send anyone searching for the his-and-hers K-Y. But what I see in that scene—what I felt as I participated in it—was an abiding sense of intimacy and love and companionship, free of pressure to be anyone other than me, just as I am, tending to what Sasha calls my girlstache. I'm with the guy I can laugh with, the guy who would find a way to tell me honestly that he thought I looked nice even if my girlstache spread up the sides of my face like a she-wolf. He loves me that much.

Paul and I haven't been together for 15 straight years. We dated after meeting that day on the train, but, hot as I was, I torched him and moved on to my long and rather silly romantic career, involving (incomplete list) a few writers, a trainer, a "branding specialist," a historian and a ballerino, several percussionists and grad students, an SAT tutoring magnate, a lighting designer, numerous journalists and at least one male nurse. (The man I opted for over Paul back then was obsessed with futzing around in a computer lab and spent most of his time on some ridiculous nascent pursuit called "the Internet and computer animation." Clearly, that was going nowhere.) Most of these guys, I recognize now, were unwitting foils to my self-discovery. I learned a lot from them, primarily how ill-prepared I was at the time to settle down myself.

Eventually, at 34, I remet Paul, at a wedding of mutual

friends, and within 18 months we were married. We are in the unique situation to have dated when we were in our mid-20s and then again when we were older. By the time we got together for keeps, both of us were fully adults, and good and set in our ways. Still, the shift to Formerly, which took place after we were married a few years, has brought subtle changes.

For me, this has mostly to do with feeling, in the words of the immortal Popeye, that I yam what I yam. I have felt this way for a long time, since before I was with my husband, but now that I'm a Formerly, it has a less defiant, defensive quality, because it no longer seems that what I am is at risk of being diminished by the man I'm with. It did back when we were first married, and it led to various territorial skirmishes. Marriage is about union, and as much as I wanted to marry Paul, I was on guard that uniting didn't mean merging and thus ceasing to exist. Now that what I am is completely mine, now that I'm completely me, that sense of self could no more get lost than my uterus could fall out from between my legs without my noticing it.

It's a relief to feel I can go about negotiating closeness with another vulnerable, imperfect human with the knowledge that who I am will not be suppressed or compromised into nothingness. That's a gift that time has given. I'm not saying that I compromise in my marriage less than I used to. In fact, I compromise more, as does my husband. Just not about who I am, something I did as unthinkingly as wearing stupid shoes when I was younger.

From my current vantage, I find some of the stuff I did in the name of love rather horrifying, but clearly, self-abnegating behavior was not my sole province. I have a newish friend, Diana, who is one of the coolest, most to-gether, non-doormat-type women I know. I guess I assumed she popped out of her mother's womb self-actualized, but that, too, seems to be a by-product of living and loving for as long as we have. One thing she admitted she did reminded me of the type of advice I read in women's magazines when I was a teenager: "Guys like girls who share their interests, so act interested!" When, at 25, Diana first started dating the man who later became her husband, she professed an all-consuming passion for mountain-biking, because he men-tioned that he liked it. She then dropped $1,500 for a mountain bike to join him on the trails. It wasn't until after they'd been together for a couple of years that she felt com-fortable saying that not only did she not enjoy mountain-biking, but that it did a real number on her pubic bone. "I treated dating like a job interview—I didn't know at the in-terview if I wanted the job, but I acted *as if* because I wanted the offer," she told me. The bike's now on Craigslist, along with, no doubt, countless other objects other Formerlies have decided are no longer necessary to further their pur-poses. Knowing Diana, she'll probably spend the money she makes on something she really enjoys, like a spa day.

What I did when I was in my 20s was similar to Diana: I was all too quick to hand over aspects of myself for the sake of whatever relationship I was in. I didn't have a strong enough sense of myself to stand firm for what I wanted—indeed, sometimes I didn't even think to *ask* myself what I wanted. I'd let the guy set the terms—how serious things were, how often we'd see each other—as if I were completely flexible. I wasn't, but I was afraid my need was too vast, too off-putting to express. It was only after he was on the hook that I allowed myself to examine my catch. As often as not, I'd realize he wasn't such a catch after all and I'd throw him back, apparently inexplicably, twitching as he hit the water. Not that I understood any of this at the time; I mostly just walked around bewildered, hurting people or getting hurt, and then doing it again. For years there were entire neighborhoods of New York City I'd have to avoid, for fear of running into one of my ex-fish. Now I can see that I didn't know myself well enough to share myself.

Later, in my early 30s, I maybe overcorrected a little—I had a brief hard-ass phase, during which I carried a figurative "what I'm looking for" checklist on a clipboard—before doing what most people do: muddle through figuring out how to be part of a pair in love and still be yourself. Eventually I got together with Paul. And now in the Formerly years, since my sense of who I am feels less tenuous and less assailed and more of a simple fact of life, I rarely need to defend it against perceived onslaughts. In our case, it makes it easier to see the other person's point of view.

Like, I'm much more open than Paul is. Just ask and you'll know which medications I've taken, whether I'm currently in therapy and why I prefer Playtex to o.b. tampons. OK,

maybe not the last one, but you get the idea. I can't be bothered to keep things I'm not ashamed of a secret, and it seems
to make other people more comfortable talking about
sometimes taboo stuff, too. Years ago, Paul would grimace
when I spoke about personal things at a party, and later, in
the car home say, "Do you really think you should have said
that?" I'd get defensive and say, "Obviously I thought I
should say that because I DID say it." I'd then lay out my case
for why what I said was fine and how I'm a highly socially
successful human being and have rarely offended anyone,
and what the hell, did I have to act like the Queen of En-
gland, for chrissakes, and who appointed him my personal
censor, anyway?

I felt as if he was saying that my entire personality was
wrong and offensive and that he needed me to be someone
else. If such an exchange were to happen now (which it
likely wouldn't because he's used to my big mouth and trusts
me not to reveal his private affairs, like the time he—Just
kidding!), I'd simply raise an eyebrow at him. I know I am
less private than him—than most people, in fact—but it
works for me. If what I say sometimes embarrasses him, it
means he has a lower threshold for public revelation than I
do, not that I'm a big boorish (Formerly Hot) mess. When
I look at it that way, I don't feel as defensive, and I'm able to
be sensitive to his discomfort and maybe not go into my
whole birth control history with his mother.

Of course, this level of understanding could simply be because I've been married for a while now, and I feel more se-

cure. It's hard to tease out what changes in a relationship are due to being a wise Formerly and which are due to simply having figured out the best way not to act on the impulse to grab a letter opener and inflict multiple puncture wounds on one's partner (not that I've ever thought about that). I know for me, nowadays, the more "right" I think I am, the less I need to fight about it and get my husband to agree with me.

Another friend of mind, Jenna, who has been married 10 years, has come to something similar. "Before, it wasn't so much that I needed to be RIGHT as that I felt like we needed to agree—that it was fundamental to our relationship. How can I live with a man forever who thinks THIS while I think THAT???" Today Jenna gives less of a hoot what people in general think of her, and that includes her husband, in the best possible way. "When we fight," she says, "I think we both mostly just want to be heard. If I get that from him, I don't need to agree or be right." Personally, I find that yelling ensures you get heard, so that's my first resort. Kidding. Another thing I've learned: The opposite is true.

I love being married to my husband, in particular, but if God forbid something were to happen to him, I highly doubt I'd do it again. For one thing, my husband has ruined me for anyone else—I can't imagine another man trying as hard to make me happy or being as patient with my faults. But the big reason is that marriage breaks your balls. It's far harder than parenthood, at least for me. Sarah, divorced when she was 32, is dating, but with no real urgency or momentum. And while she'd like to meet someone—regular sex is something she misses, the man hunt is not the all-consuming focus of her limited free time, as it might be for someone who has never been married. This is partly because at 43 she's reconciled to not having biological children, and so has no deadlines to beat.

Being a Formerly usually means that your life experience has disabused you of any romantic fantasies of being whisked away from the icky parts of life, least of all by another person, let alone one on a white steed. "Having been married, I know that there's nothing magical about it—there's nothing that's going to magically change when you say 'I do,' " Sarah explained. No joke. After having slogged through some of the harder times in my marriage, I've come to the same conclusion. In fact, you only become more yourself the longer you're with someone, and this realization—that real life is not always as sparkly as the kind of fantasies I had about love when I was younger—is richer and more reliable. As Sarah put it (I swear the girl should be an oracle, or at least a life coach): "I know that whether I'm alone or with a partner, I'll have joys and disappointments. They'll be different ones if I'm not with someone, but they won't be fewer." I do believe she's right.

If a single Formerly actively wants a partner, of course, the apparent dearth of decent men doesn't make it easy. It's a nationwide mystery and a source of endless speculation where the ones who aren't married, aren't fatally flawed and are looking to be in a relationship congregate. The romantic possibilities don't feel endless, as they did when we were all in college. Another friend of mine, let's call her Helene, has been divorced for five years and is dating in earnest. She told me, with a roll of her eyes, "Instead of asking a guy where he lives or where he went to summer camp, it is more like, When you say you're separated, does that mean you still live with your wife and you just don't sleep with her anymore?" Part of what's tough about it is that many people are paired off, or there's a glaring reason they're not. Not to mention that guys date down in terms of age, whereas, cougar stereotype to the contrary, women generally prefer their more mature peers.

But back to Sarah. Spending time with her and hearing her opinions on the various men she has dated recently has made me aware of something that may explain the relative dearth of decent guys at our age: an unwillingness to bend to the point of discomfort, to, say, become involved in a relationship that requires you to change your already jampacked, lovely, rich life too much. She is the walking, talking, good-life-living embodiment of what makes being this age so wonderful—knowing yourself, not caring much what others think, and a hard-won sense of confidence and independence. But needing so little can make remaining unattached way more appealing than trying to cram a round relationship into a square hole. There's no moving to Pittsburgh for a year while he finishes med school, and there's no being with someone you hope will improve with time. Sarah said: "Things work really well now, and there is so much that's fulfilling to me already, so to bring someone into my life, he has to add to it." Sarah inspires the hell out of me, even though I am married.

The truth is, I always thought the people I was with when I was younger added to my life—why would anyone go out with someone who doesn't? It was just that the specific things they added—drama, intensity, wild anecdotes I could share about the things they wanted me to call them in bed— weren't what I needed, and it took me a long time to realize that. Many of the men I dated, of course, were wonderful, but the good things they contributed weren't enough to balance out what I felt they were taking away. Now that we're all older, we want a lot from the people we're with, because in many ways we need less. After a date with a perfectly nice guy, in which she came away with a vague sense of why his last relationship didn't work out, Sarah said, "I am not willing to commit to someone's potential anymore." The handful of friends I know who have gotten separated or divorced have done so because the guy they thought they'd married didn't live up to his potential, and being alone (and free to look for someone else) was preferable.

Lest this sounds like the guy needs to be perfect, that's not what I mean. I never thought I'd be married to a guy who eats all but one bite of cottage cheese and puts it back in the fridge, because—my theory—being the kind of guy who snarfs all the cottage cheese doesn't fit in with his self-image. (Of course, I don't realize we're out until it's too late for me to get any.) Knowing your own foibles can make you more tolerant of others', and I know I do things he finds equally irritating. Shocking, I know.

But we're talking foibles, not major obstacles to being a successful human being—such as having a primary care doctor, an income or a viable plan for generating one, or being able to accept that if, by age 42, his band hasn't broken through, then making music is merely a fun hobby—that a guy isn't taking responsibility for. I love the way Sarah explains it (clearly she's devoted no small amount of thought to this): "We're at midlife, so he needs to be at least midway toward living the kind of life he wants." Given the number of guys she eschews, that would seem to mean she has high standards, but it doesn't sound that way to me.

The flip side of having such a full life without a partner is that it can be hard to clear out emotional closet space for one. But having been around the block more than your average 25-year-old makes it easier to spot the right person when he does happen by (and friends tell me that you have fewer superficial deal-breakers, like he must surpass your height in heels by at least two inches). That's what happened with my never-married friend Andrea, who last year, after much dating, finally met her life partner. She knows he's right for her because "In every relationship I was in, I would jump through a million hoops to make it work," she told me. Her guy fits into her life and she to his—she needn't change hers in ways that are important to her for the sake of staying together. Now she knows that while relationships take work, "Not everything needs to feel like work. Your life should

feel like it's opening a bit because of this person, not closing."

I feel lucky to have realized this in my 30s, and so knew
to grab Paul when I had the (second) opportunity. And with
him I feel like my life is opening. And that's why we're still
together—that, and the fact that at this age, I know it's
mostly my job to keep my own life feeling full of possibility.
I think that's why Sarah is happy, despite not having met the
right guy. "I want to meet someone, yes, but I want a lot of
things." She shrugs. "It's kind of a relief—if you've got the
resources to have a happy life, you will have one. It's nice
being less invested in the outcome."

Not every Formerly is so circumspect, of course. Some
single women feel as if it's now or never, and the married
ones are sometimes not content with their lot. After a few
drinks, I know more than a few women who fret half-
jokingly that they can't believe their husbands are the last
people they're ever going to have sex with. To borrow a
phrase from *He's Not That Into You,* they don't want to "waste
their pretty" on the men they married! They say, "I look
good now, and that won't last forever, so if I'm going to
cheat, I'd better get on it." They are mostly kidding, of
course, but some probably feel like a part of their lives that
they miss is being closed off by their relationships, or in
some way the relationship is not doing it for them. That
happens, especially because what you and your partner (who
is probably also hitting Formerly right about now) need can
change over time. No amount of hard-won wisdom and ma-

turity can protect you from shit happening, or from the fact that unless you're Julia Child (who—according to the movie *Julie and Julia*, anyway—had one of those rare, enviable marriages in which she and her husband only found each other more endearingly quirky over time), spending every day with the same, imperfect person can sometimes be . . . just what it is.

But knowing yourself, and knowing what you need, gives you a huge leg up when it comes to love, and keeps you from bailing at the first or 15th sign of blah-ness. Amy jokingly bemoaned the tepid romance in her marriage, but then clarified: "I used to think romance was important. Now I know that having a guy who will—without any whining whatsoever—go without sleep all night to stay up with you when you've had a horrible sinus surgery and will then drive you to the hospital in the morning in a snowstorm so they can fix it, that's what's important."

That, and someone who thinks you're sexy even with moustache bleach on your lip.

R.I.P. the Imposter

knew something had changed for me at work when, one afternoon a couple of years ago, I walked down the hallway to my office, balancing my drink on my sandwich and stabilizing the whole setup with my chin as I slid open my office door. I was working then at a magazine at which I managed a group of junior editors, whose cubicles were in a row outside my office. Three of them were huddled around one of their computer monitors, not an uncommon sight around the features department, where people often help one another with tricky on-screen issues. I smiled and raised my eyebrows at them as I bumped open the door with my hip, to acknowledge how goofy I must have looked. They smiled back. After setting my lunch down on my messy desk, I realized I'd forgotten to take a straw. I stuck my head out of my office, preparing to ask if anyone had a spare.

"Hey, guys," I said. As soon as I spoke, all three of them swooshed their heads 180 degrees away from the computer toward me, seemingly startled. They wore identical half smiles and wide, surprised eyes.

"Sorry—does anyone have a straw?" One scooted to her desk and another fumbled in drawers—a bit too solicitously, in my view. I glanced at the screen, and noticed, underneath a few windows with legitimate-looking documents and websites in them, one web page with rows of shoes peaking out. It was obviously Zappos. If we were in a silent movie, there would be an organ chord heralding the moment of discovery that just took place.

The thing is, I couldn't care less. Those young women worked like Oompa-Loompas well into the evening, whereas I had long since realized that there was very little that couldn't wait until the next morning, or come home with me at 5:30 if truly critical. I would never have be-grudged them a little personal time at work. I was a bit . . . not stung, exactly, but surprised. They were hiding Zappos from me, of all people? Surely they'd seen the blue, black and white Zappos boxes arriving almost monthly at my office! I said nothing. If I had spoken, the only thing I would have said was "Cute boots," because they *were* cute, but I didn't want them to have to stammer an unnecessary explanation. I got a straw, and went back into my cave.

As I ate lunch, I thought about it. I realized I couldn't re-member the last time they opened their clusters to include me in their conversations about recalcitrant boyfriends or their favorite reality shows. We had a nice rapport, and they seemed to feel comfortable speaking their minds about work matters around me, but clearly, I was not one of them. When had *that* happened? The fact that I wouldn't have minded if they ordered shoes from their desk was completely irrelevant. The point was, they saw me as someone who *might* mind, and that's what put me in a different class of workplace denizen. Just as my tween and teen nieces and nephews look at me as a "cool" adult but with narc potential, I had become a "cool" boss, but a boss nonetheless.

It didn't seem too terribly long ago that I was one of those women, shiny, taut-skinned and eager to please, striving with a smile, even as I was outrageously underpaid. When I was 22 and an assistant at a magazine, I smuggled toilet paper from the ladies' room home in my purse each week, in part because I was broke, and also because I felt somewhat ill-used. But that was as subversive as I allowed myself to be. Otherwise I was a good puppy, volunteering for the extra-credit projects and laboring over a six-word caption for half a day, grateful for the opportunity to do so.

The captions quickly became blurbs and then stories and features, but over the years my attitude remained the same. I was the goodest girl among the good girls magazine publishing tends to attract. I never said no, no matter how silly or doomed to fail I could foresee a project was, and I was conscientious in the extreme. This all made me very successful, if you define success in terms of raises and promotions and TV spots and parties and making a name for oneself relatively young.

Most people would define success that way. I certainly did, but in the last decade or so I realized that definition was not entirely suiting me. The rumblings of a shift began when I was around 31, and the second-in-command at *Glamour* magazine. We were closing (that's when all futzing over fonts and facts ceases and the pages of a magazine leave the building one by one to go to the printer), and it was a wicked closing—some stories had come in late, some had legal problems and our editor-in-chief had made countless last-minute changes, which meant that a large crew of us were working late nights. I caught a glimpse of myself from above, as if I were not me, but me looking at a nannycam video of me. What I saw was pretty gross.

There I was, my hair frizzy and twisted up with a pencil, circles under my eyes, scarfing sushi in the back of a Town Car at midnight on my way home from the office for the third night in a row. The corporately funded Dragon Roll had been on my desk since seven, when those of us working late had ordered in. I had meant to eat it, but every time I was about to snap the takeout chopsticks apart, a page proof would land on my desk or someone needed me to weigh in on a decision. I'd hop up and put productivity and good nature before my own growling tummy. That resulted in me, five hours later, being driven home in a luxury company car, one in which Anna Wintour herself, the sleek and coiffed editor of *Vogue,* might have sat in earlier in the evening. I was dripping soy sauce on the sushi from a plastic packet, trying not to splash it on the plush leather upholstery.

Behold, the lowest moment of my fabulous career as a glamorous magazine editor: The raw fish was at room temperature. I knew I should chuck it. I gave it a sniff. It smelled OK. I paused. I was so ravenous that, yes, I ate it, forcing from my mind's eye all images of the microscopic larval worms that might be squiggling through the little slabs of tuna. There was a tiny, self-protective part of my psyche shouting inaudibly like the Who to Horton: YOU'RE AN IDIOT! DON'T EAT THE FISH! ANNA WINTOUR WOULD NEVER EAT THE FISH! I could barely hear it then. I think that whispering speck of wisdom and dignity was secretly hoping I'd spend the night bent over the toilet puking my lungs up so I would have to take the next day off.

I didn't get sick, but something clicked that night, like a light switch turning off, and for the first time, the phrase "work-life balance" felt meaningful to me. I knew I had to dial it back, and thought that simply meant working less and leaving earlier. And I did so as often as I could bring myself to. Whenever I lapsed into disgusting habits borne of overwork I'd mentally recite my new mantra: *Anna Wintour wouldn't eat the fish,* and that kept me on track. To an extent.

Setting limits and saying no to work proved terribly difficult for me, and in the process of trying to live saner I slowly realized why: I believed—despite the awards I'd won for my writing and editing and the fact that I was sought after in my field—that the only reason anyone kept me around was because they liked me. Some irrational part of me felt that if my relentlessly good attitude soured or if I had a bad day, I would be out on my keister. It was absurd and there was zero evidence for the theory, but that's how I'd operated for years. In retrospect, I cannot believe how much of my success at work I attributed primarily to my personality.

Of course, it never hurts to be liked. If an employer has to choose between two people with identical abilities, the one who is perkier, more compliant, works until nine and who keeps a bowl of M&M's on her desk has the edge over the surly, resentful one who rolls his eyes and heaves great sighs when charged with a task. But the problem with the extent to which I took being liked was that if most of my value was in how others felt about me personally, I was at the mercy of their opinions. Following this logic, the quality of my work (which, after all, was what I was being paid for) meant very little. I knew I was talented, but not enough, I thought, to permit me to be human.

Anyone who has ever watched *Dr. Phil* could deduce that I had issues with authority growing up—more specifically, abandonment issues, which is probably why I felt like I had to be a perfect little pom-pom girl at the office or I'd be out peddling matches on a cold winter's night. But these days, perhaps because I've been The Man at work (though I, too, am working for The Man every night and day) and at least theoretically an authority figure at home, those issues no longer play themselves out in the workplace. My superiors at work are just that—my superiors at work, people who, by dint of the various choices they made and their ability and experience, are in the position to get me and others to do their bidding. It's like when my twin girls play house, and one is the older sister and the other the baby—they agree to certain roles and abide by them. They don't get all twisted up about the unfairness of it all, because it's really just a game, and they go back to their old relationship when it's over. These days, work is something of a game—one that, between nine and five or six, I take as seriously as those dark-souled guys who played Dungeons & Dragons in junior high, but a game nonetheless. When I'm the boss, which I have been on and off over the years, I feel that Level III Grand Wizard Overlord, or whatever, is my role for the moment, not my entire identity. It makes me less intense about the whole career thing.

Just so you know, the sushi revelation was hardly sweeping, and did not instantly turn me into a wiser, more Zen person who took excellent care of her physical and emotional health. Even today, I sometimes sit and write until my butt falls asleep and I have to stand up until it stops tingling. Praise from a boss still warms me and makes me feel secure. But gradually I became less invested in other people's opinions, in a good way. In caring less about how I'm perceived, I follow my own instincts, rather than aiming for what I think would please, which means I often do better work. It sure beats living in self-imposed insecurity. Through finding that I didn't get shit-canned if I showed up unprepared to the occasional meeting or opted out of a project entirely, I began to know—really know, not just intellectually—that my worth at work isn't so tenuous.

I am still occasionally surprised that no one has noticed that my people-pleaser button is permanently broken. There are days when I feel as if I'm slacking off, or that my head is back at kindergarten drop-off, where my daughter Vivian wouldn't let go of my hand, and no one notices or cares. It just reinforces the fact that my expectations of myself when I was younger were off the charts. Now not only can I state my opinion with the confidence that I know what I'm talking about, but I have leeway to be outwardly grumpy, petty and exasperated every so often, which is critical to my mental health. I am no longer capable of keeping a lid on negative emotions indefinitely.

Oh, and I can afford toilet paper now, the good kind, not the scratchy, one-ply commercial-issue kind.

Having other demands on my time, such as a family or a compelling interest in things other than work, which you're more likely to develop as you get older, further complicates the life-balance issue. It's a toughie, and the "you can have it all" line of crap that women my age grew up with doesn't help. Next to the block-print letters "YOU CAN HAVE IT ALL!!!" (three exclamation points, always three) on the banner waved at us by our parents and popular culture and the commencement speaker at our graduation, there is an almost microscopic asterisk. When you find its mate at the bottom of the flag, there is a list of caveats, written in mouse print, that is as long as my arm.

YOU CAN HAVE IT ALL!!!★

★Some restrictions apply. Not available in all areas or to all socioeconomic groups. Void where prohibited by law. "All" includes unlimited guilt for never feeling as if you're giving anything its proper attention. In having it "All," we make no representation that you will have enough of any of it, or that having it "All" will make you happy. By that we mean that while you may have a relationship, you will likely be unable to nurture it; you may have children, but you will almost certainly not see them as much as you would like; you will have money, yet you will never feel as if you have quite enough. Your plants will die (even the spider plant the florist assured you was unkillable) because you're too tired from having it "All" to water them. You will be ignorant of the important matters facing your nation because you haven't read a newspaper in forever. We are not liable for any slip-and-fall accidents that result from your marbles spilling out of your head and onto the floor, and waive any responsibility for the losses and/or damage having it "All" might cause to yourself and your loved ones. You should give it "All" up and contact a health-care provider immediately if agitation, depressed mood, changes in behavior or thinking that is not typical for you is observed, or if you develop suicidal ideation or suicidal behavior. In short, you may feel like shit, and wonder what's wrong with you that you need an anti-depressant just to drag your ass out of bed in the morning, because doesn't everyone want it "All"? And that's not our fault.

When I had my daughters six years ago, I did manage to have it "All" for a couple of years (the intense, high-octane job; the husband; the rewards of parenthood and the gym membership) and I've never been so miserable. Having it "All" turned me into a guilt-wracked, short-tempered zombie with a dried-up raisin for a brain.

Here's an example of how having it "All" can turn you into someone you hate: One winter morning, my husband and the girls and I were in the elevator of our apartment building, rushing out to preschool drop-off. After that, I was to shoot uptown on the train to my office, along the way grabbing breakfast and dropping off prescriptions and buying baby shampoo and diapers to schlep home that evening, and my mind was churning with all I had to do. Paul was holding Sasha, red-faced and dripping with boogers, still crying over a toy I said she couldn't bring. I had Vivian, bloated to twice her size in her pink down puffer jacket, who was clutching a waffle with peanut butter, and making little brown handprints on my (beige!) shearling coat. Sweat ran down my lower back into my waistband, I had to pee and my head was throbbing because I hadn't had my coffee yet.

The elevator stopped on another floor, which, in my crabbiness, made me inordinately annoyed—as if it were my private express elevator—and then made me feel selfish and guilty for feeling that way. A well-meaning, elderly neighbor got on, and smiled, looked at the drippy Sasha and a peanut–butter covered Vivian and evidently saw this as the perfect moment to say, "Enjoy every minute with them while they're young, because they get older so fast!"

I seriously wanted to punch him, although of course it wasn't his fault. Tone-deaf as his comment was (I don't know any parent who would have enjoyed that sticky, screechy elevator ride), it shined a white-hot spotlight on the fact that I wasn't even enjoying the pleasant, loving, truly joyous moments as much as I might have if I hadn't been exhausted and driven witless by too many details swimming around my malnourished, anxious brain. I walked around all day, every day, feeling thick with guilt, remiss and impure, as if anything I did, no matter how necessary or worthwhile, was stealing time from something else I should have been doing. It wasn't that anyone—my kids, my bosses, my husband—was demanding more of me than they had a right to. It was all just too much.

When the girls were four, I hit a wall and saw that I had to give up at least some of it to make my life more manageable. Everyone exhibits different symptoms of Having It All syndrome, and here are a few of mine, aside from the aforementioned urge to punch old people.

- You look like crap.
- You feel even worse.
- You do most of your food shopping at convenience stores—mmm, mini rice cakes and Kraft Singles for dinner!—because you can't get to the supermarket before it closes.

- You are irked when you receive a wedding invitation, because weddings take, like, all damn day! If you're asked to be in a wedding, you feel that the bride is genuinely inconsiderate.

- When a friend suggests that you take some time for yourself, you laugh ruefully. How naïve can one woman be?

- You say diva-esque things that would normally never come out of your mouth, like "In what universe would I have time for this?!" and "I'm sorry, but that's unacceptable," to members of your own family.

- You fall asleep while playing Sleeping Beauty with your kids and they grow hysterical because their magical kiss of true love fails to awaken you.

- You break down in tears because the icing on the carrot cake that you ordered for dessert on the one date night you and your husband have in four months is butter-, not cream cheese–based. "It's like, I. Just. Wanted. Cream cheese. Frosting. Why is that so hard? Is that so much to ask? SOB!"

- You become livid when your husband suggests that maybe it's not about the frosting.

- You hate your husband.

- You have aphasia for common words, including your beloved children's names.

- It doesn't matter, because you kind of hate them, too.

- But not as much as you hate their babysitter, who gets to spend way more time with your kids than you do.

- You're sort of glad your office has no window so you won't see that it's nice out.

You can see why I quit my very intense job and took another that was three days a week so I could order bits and pieces of it "All" à la carte, instead of trying to force down the Have It All deluxe platter. Friends at work said I was "brave" for "choosing" to scale back, after I'd achieved so much and may not be able to resume my career at the same level if I someday wanted to. I didn't feel brave, and I didn't feel as if I'd had a choice. I felt like I was losing my shit.

It was an adjustment. Adrenaline continued to course through my veins at the same breakneck speed as it had when I needed it to propel me through my day, even though my days were considerably less demanding. At first I didn't know what to do with the extra electric energy. The first evening after I left my new office and headed to the train, by habit I began mentally plotting the route home and the errands I could knock off along the way—what did I need at the drugstore by the subway, the supermarket on our corner, did we have anything at the dry cleaners, takeout for dinner?—before I realized that I didn't *have* to do anything but go home and see my girls. For once, there was nothing that couldn't wait a day or two, because my life now included time in which nothing was scheduled. It was a strange feeling, not simply going from chore to event to obligation, and it made me a little anxious, but at the same time it was nice. I knew I'd done the right thing.

After a couple of months of decompressing, success for me began to include the luxury of being able to finish a thought, watching my girls in ballet class without thinking of the messages I had to return and remembering why I married my husband. I could also sleep at night, and I became a better friend, because I wasn't surreptitiously ordering groceries from an online food delivery service while on the phone, supposedly helping them process their deepest anxieties. It was only then that I realized I didn't even want it "All."

It was hard giving up a huge, important job, though, with the title and the money that came with it. I loved the job that I quit, and I missed being in charge of people who might actually listen to me, as opposed to my kids, who took their orders from SpongeBob. I missed being able to sum up my identity on a business card and slide it across the table, and I missed having the recipient automatically understand that I was someone to take seriously. All those things left a huge career-gal-shaped hole where they used to be. It was difficult to will myself not to care too much about what went down at my new, part-time job, because as a consultant, it was no longer my place to do so. I had to remind myself that I chose this new way of doing things, and that being a less important person in the work world didn't mean I was in fact a less important human being.

At the same time, though, I felt more relaxed and able to meet the new expectations I'd set for myself, and because of that I did not feel any less successful in life. In fact,

I felt more so. In my case, not being able to have it "All" simply meant that there were too many good things for me to choose from, and I had to be selective for the sake of my sanity. I didn't see it as a failure, although I know some do.

I saw a bumper sticker once that said, "If at first you don't succeed, lower your standards!" It cracked me up, because I live and die by that motto at home. If I can't get the nail out of the wall without making the hole bigger, I hang a picture over the nail and call it a job well done. Resisting the "having it all" mind-set, I found, can't be seen as settling for less. I think that's more about being freethinking enough to decide what success means to you, and not buying in to the easiest, quickest definition, the only one that presented itself to me when I was young. Just as there is more than one definition of "hot," but you don't find that out until you no longer fit the most obvious one, there is more than one definition of "success," which you can only appreciate when you've lived long enough to have tried a few things on for size.

Success to me for now means thriving in my little niche of the work world, raising kids who are smart and kind and finding a way to laugh several times a day, rather than being a big name high on a masthead. My definition of "success" wouldn't do it for everyone, of course. It all depends where you started. Strangely, even as well as I did at work, I was never particularly ambitious. I was driven more by the need for a pat on the head than fame or money. I would think that achieving career success might be harder if you have the kind of concrete hopes and dreams that you are led to believe should be attainable in a linear progression. If you do X, Y and Z, and you want it badly enough, you can be what you want to be. That was never the way I thought, and it is very often not the case, which can be a blow if you're a Formerly who has done everything right.

The other day I ran into an old friend, Karen, who mentioned a guy she'd set me up with when I was around 25. John was gorgeous—tall, thin, with high, planar cheekbones and long, dark, potential rock-star hair. He was, in fact, a potential rock star, hoping, strategizing and even *planning* on how his life would be different once he broke through. I'd never heard him play, but in terms of the look, he was good to go. I thought he was incredibly hot, and found his dreams for the future charming, if a bit impractical.

The spark got snuffed out over Italian food, when he asked me what my dreams were. "I don't know . . . I'd definitely like to get a raise or a better-paying job so I can get a place of my own," I replied. I was freelancing at a tabloid newspaper at the time, and doing little pieces here and there in magazines. He wasn't buying it, and pressed me for what he felt sure was my *real* dream, the one that would presumably provide insight into my true self. "Come on," I remember him saying. "You must have something you really, really want to do." I told him I didn't have a gigantic, sparkly, long-term dream like his, that I was more of a follow-the-happiness, day-to-day kind of gal. As I said it, it sounded unromantic even to me, but it was the truth. I worked at magazines and newspapers, and really wanted to do well, but had no ambitions to run one. I worked with words, but didn't think of myself as an artist. Such ideas and definitions would occasionally shoot through me, but they never seemed to take hold. They all felt grandiose.

He shook his head in a mixture of disbelief and resignation. "You have to have a dream, Stephanie. You need to dream bigger."

Wow, did I ever feel like a big old loser at that moment. At 25, part of me thought he was right, that there was something wrong with me for having such low expectations of life. Didn't everyone have some lofty aspiration? If I didn't, how would I ever fulfill my potential, whatever that was?

At 42, it's a question I still ask, but am too busy to spend much time pondering. I have a remarkable husband and two scary-smart little girls who awe me every day with how their little lawyer minds work. I have a job with people I like and respect, an outlet in my blog and other projects, and make enough money to buy my girls the Hannah Montana microphones they crave, because their dream du jour is to be rock stars. (More like Pink than Hannah Montana, Sasha assures me.) I have friends who are extensions of my family. With the exception of an overwhelming baby jones in my early 30s, which felt more physical than anything, none of these things were particular goals of mine.

Still, they make me happy, just as I'd imagine they would

had I set them as benchmarks and then achieved them. Perhaps because I don't have pie-in-the-sky dreams, or any kind of a bucket list, I'm delighted when things go well. That's why finding success in smaller things is possible for me.

I wondered about John, though, especially when Karen said the music thing didn't really work out. We didn't have time to do a full debriefing, so I don't know what became of him. I hope that he, too, has learned to appreciate a broader-based version of success. I'll bet he has—otherwise he'd be a miserable aging rock-star wannabe, and I can't see him doing that for very long. People tend to upend themselves after a fall, even from a lofty height. A few decades on this planet makes you realize that a diversified success portfolio means that if one aspect of your life is in the shitter, you're not a total washout.

Like many graduating college seniors, I had little clue what I wanted to do with my oh-so-practical liberal arts degree. I wound up in magazines because it was the best steady paycheck I could envision that didn't require me to wear panty hose in order to earn. Magazines felt tangible to me, unlike the investment banks and large accounting firms that reached out to college seniors back in 1989 to recruit them. (Note to younger readers: Once upon a time, there were lots of investment banks, and they magically all made money.) I didn't feel as if the world was my oyster so much as there were only a handful of things I might be good at, and writing was one of them. And ever since that turned out to be the case, I have become addicted to feeling competent, in a way I never realized could be so gratifying.

Which is probably why it took me only about six days into my maternity leave to know that I didn't have what it took to be a stay-at-home mom, not that it was a real option for my family, for financial reasons. Granted, I had twins, and that was exponentially harder than I imagine it would be to have one. Still, there was no question that I could not be with the kids all day every day, at least not happily. The lack of structure combined with sheer tedium was grueling, especially on no sleep and with leaky boobs. I tried yoga to get in the live-in-the-moment mind-set, but there were no Mommy/Baby/Baby classes. Meditation was not an option; I'd fall asleep, I was so tired, only to be awoken by one or another crying infant. Xanax would have helped, but I was nursing and so thought better of it. Feeling as if I was a good mom would have required me to give up any semblance of agency and just roll with what the day brought us—the exact opposite skills that had made me so successful at work.

When I went back to work after three months, I was overjoyed to be at my desk with a coffee I could drink to the bottom while it was still hot, and full of admiration for women who could do what I couldn't. I raced home to see my babies every night (pumped milk in Baggies in a cooler), and appreciated them all the more because I had gone to work. Even now that the girls are older, parenting requires a calm and a divestment from any specific outcome, which doesn't come to me easily. I have learned to feel competent as a mom, in my own way, but I still have that "thank God it's Monday" moment when I drop them off at school. And because I'm older, and have more than one thing in my life that makes me feel successful, I feel less guilty about my need— my desire—to work.

Working-mom guilt is huge for nearly every working mom I know, of course. But while I still have some (like when one of my daughters desperately wants me to chaperone her class trip to the organic farm "like all the other mothers," and I have to say no), it's not as crippling as I imagine it would be if I were younger. All the overhyped Mommy Wars silliness feels to me more of a young woman's battle, one that's more about identity and feeling useful and successful in the world than about whether there's a "right" choice or a "right" way to raise children. I'm positive that if I'd had the girls when I was younger, and circumstances permitted me to stay home with them, I would have taken up the banner of Stay at Home Mother and used that same banner to impale anyone who sought to belittle my identity or my contribution to society as such. But as an older mom, with that diversified success portfolio, I don't feel as though I need to pick a lane. That's a delicious freedom that makes being a mom much easier.

All of this circumspection doesn't mean that women my age always feel hunky-dory about all their choices. It seems as though we're fated to fret, at least a little. My family and I spent one weekend this past summer with my friend Olivia and her crew, and once the kids were (finally) down, we got to drinking and philosophizing about life. About half a bottle of wine in, Olivia got to musing, in a big-picture kind of way: "I sometimes wonder, could I have been doing something these past years that's worthy of a couple of column inches in the *Times* when I die? I love what I do, but I'm not changing the world. I always assumed I would when I was younger, but now I think, is it going to happen on my clock?" she said. "Tick-tock, take stock."

Olivia had just had a milestone birthday—40—and so I guess was in inventory mode. Depending on when I catch her and if she's sober (which she generally is), Olivia is clear that she loves her job as a hospital administrator too much to make a switch any time soon, and would not want the kind of career that would dig into her time with her two boys. But she still wonders. "You make choices, but you can always still mourn the path you didn't take."

That's one thing I've managed not to do, so far, even after a full bottle. It appears I'm too busy mourning other things, such as my fuller head of hair and my erstwhile ability to pick up men on the subway. When I'm feeling good, which is most of the time, I focus on the choices I've made that brought me to where I am now, which is to say, feeling good most of the time. As long as I keep my eyes on the prize—remaining happy, helping my family and loved ones to feel likewise, and earning enough to cover what is truly needed—I expect to look back at a successful life career. Rather than asking myself *What would Anna Wintour do?* I can ask myself, *What would* I *do?* and know that I'll likely hit on the right answer for me. And just knowing that I will never again feel the need to steal toilet paper from the corporate restroom or to eat warm sushi in a moving vehicle makes me feel as if I've achieved a lot.

20

The Formerly Purge

've done a few closet purges in the last couple of years, with my Formerly friend Rhonda sitting by to make sure I don't cave in and keep everything, as well as to remind me of the nuttier things I did while wearing some of the clothes I'm donating. There's a touch of the bittersweet, like when I'm reminded how intensely I felt for the guy I was dancing with at a particular bar in a particular pair of sandals. I then remember the blisters I had the next day and the agony I felt the next week when he didn't call and I stalked him like the insecure hot mess that I was, and I'm happy to give them to Goodwill. Rhonda and I laugh, are grateful that we're not young and raw anymore, and we move on to the next item.

These are some of the questions I ask Rhonda to ask me when we do the Formerly Purge.

1. Does it fit? If it causes me any pain—and that includes emotional pain at the sight of my flesh oozing over my

waistband—I know what I have to do. Yes, even if I can button it. Yes, even if it was expensive. Yes, even if it's nominally my size. I should be able to wear it comfortably, so I can breathe and bend my extremities.

2. Can I sit and pick something up from the floor in it without my ass showing? If not, are there any occasions at which I'd *want* my ass to show? How often do I expect to be engaging in activities in which I'd want my ass to show? Not often? I need to get rid of it.

3. Did it ever look good? Sometimes I buy things and grow to hate them but keep them out of principle to remind myself what an idiot I was to buy them in the first place. There is no room for useless self-recrimination in the life of a Formerly. Nothing good ever comes of it. Buh-bye!

4. Does it have any writing on it? Labels and writing that is incorporated into graphics are exceptions, but by and large, a Formerly doesn't need her T-shirt to do the talking for her. That shirt that said, "I'm hotter than your girlfriend," that someone gave you probably isn't going to get a lot of wear.

5. Does it have a tear, run or split seam that I've been meaning to get repaired for years? I'll take it out of the closet, put it in my bag and see if I actually stop at the tai-

lor. If I don't, I don't hang it back up for later. Out it goes. Life's too short to have stuff like this hanging over your head.

6. Does it have classic potential? A trench coat, a leopard-print jacket, a pair of dark denim jeans, a well-cut blazer. Even if I haven't worn these in a few years, I hang on to them. I can always reevaluate later.

I'm happy to say that I am no longer in a state of fashion emergency, now that I have better choices, wisdom and, of course, more of a facility with all things Formerly. I am often still late for getting my daughters to school, but this is now their getting-dressed issue, not mine. *I* get dressed every morning with new clothing and mix in a few old standbys that I think will always work for me. I haven't missed any-thing I've given away—well, maybe that leather skirt, just a bit, even though it was too short—because hanging on to outdated clothing can be just as stultifying as clinging to an identity or a lifestyle that doesn't work for you anymore. If you do that, you become another version of THOSE women (Google "Joan Van Ark images" and you'll see what I mean), and frankly, I'd rather be me.

21

Formerly a Formerly

About ten years ago, right around the time I got engaged to my husband, I was having coffee with a good girlfriend. Let's call her Jackie. She and I had spent countless hours over the years trying to solve such nuanced relationship issues as to whether a guy who cheats on his girlfriend with you could ever be faithful to you, should you and he get together for real; if you really like a guy but despise his '70s cop moustache, how long you have to wait to say something; and what the fact that he lives in a studio with nothing but a single bed and a stack of take-out menus might reveal about his long-term partnership capability. We had been sisters in singledom.

That crisp autumn day, Jackie was meticulously trying to tease out any potential speck of meaning that there may or may not have been in an interaction she'd had recently with an ex. She'd run into him unexpectedly on the street.

"I mean, when he said it was good to see me, did he mean, good to see me, as in, *Hey, good to see you,* or do you think he meant it, like, *It was really good to see you and I'm having pangs of regret?* I *did* look good that day, thank God. Not that I'd get back with him, but you know what I mean." I said I didn't know how he meant it, because I wasn't there, and I wasn't in his head.

"Well, he said it like, 'It's good to *see* you,' with the emphasis on 'see.' I think if he was like, 'It's good to see *you*,' he would have meant *me*, it was good to see *me*. The way he said it, it sounded just, like, friendly. Oh, God, I don't know. What do you think?" I replied something about it not really mattering, since she didn't want to get back with him anyway, so who cared what he meant?

This went on for maybe 45 minutes. During that time we covered whether he was still seeing the woman he was rumored to have been seeing after they'd broken up, what would *definitely* have to change if my friend was to take him back, if his saying "Good to see you" was, in fact, an indication that he wanted to reunite and myriad other possibilities and eventualities and hypotheticals. I had a flash of us in a comic strip, a drawing of two well-dressed chicks at a café table. Jackie's voice bubble, filled with teeny-tiny type, was taking up our entire square.

Finally, I couldn't stand it anymore. I thought she was being ridiculous, whipping a five-word comment into a giant, frothy meringue of meaning. "Jackie, here's what I think: I think if he does want to see you again, he'll call you," I snapped. "That'll be your answer! Or if you want to, you can call him and see what's up. Either way, if it's going to be something, it will, and if it won't, it won't."

I instantly regretted being so sharp. Jackie looked stung, and then started casting her eyes about for the creamer. I stammered an apology and said that it was just, I don't know, I had a lot going on, with work and planning the wedding and everything, and she didn't ask me about any of that. She said it was OK, and that she was sorry, too, but I could tell it wasn't OK, not totally. After that, and especially after Paul and I got married, things were never the same. We saw each other less and less.

The thing is, a few years earlier, it could just have easily been me on the Jackie end of that conversation, or if it had been her, I would have been totally into holding a tuning fork to the timbre of his every utterance. It was part of understanding what was going on around us, and working through our single-gal stuff. Nothing had changed in our dynamic, except my outlook and where I was in my life. After getting together with Paul, and having it work out so straightforwardly, it was clear to me that examining the minutiae of male-female interactions only got you so far and that with time (and usually not that much of it) everything becomes clear. I didn't need to fill my brain up with froth, because I had more solid things to think about. In short, I was done with all that. And just like when a smoker quits smoking, the smell of smoke becomes more irritating to her than to someone who never smoked, so were these kinds of conversations.

I get the exact same impatient, "grow up and get over it already" kind of response from some of the older women I speak to about the shock and unsettled feelings I've had

throughout this process of aging out of young. In the com-
ments on my blog posts, as well as when I just get going on
the subject at a party, some of them see my focus on the tiny,
subtle changes in my looks, my outlook and my relationships
as tedious and whiney, especially when I rant about the negative ones. I posted about when Sasha pointed out my "girlstache," the one I thought I had eradicated through various
painful means in my 20s. "All that frettin' is terribly unat-
tractive," one woman in her 50s wrote on my blog. "Definitely not hot." Her feeling is that she gets hotter every year,
and that I was putting myself and other women down by
calling myself "formerly hot." (Trying to explain that you're
being ironic kind of kills the joke, so I gave up.)

They've been there and back, and from their perspective,
I just don't get it, "it" being whatever bigger-picture outlook
they've come to develop in the years since they were Formerlies, going through what I am. Some of them may simply not have felt the Formerly shift as acutely as I do, and
many of those who did don't remember it. In any case, they
seem to have found their new balance in the world, and re-
alizing that you're suddenly no longer young and no longer
treated in the same way by the world is not something that
affects them day to day.

In truth, I appreciate the fact that some older women
readers think my priorities are misplaced (although if I have
to make it clear one more time that, yes, I still consider myself hot, just not in the same way, I think I'll just go ahead
and make "Currently Hot" T-shirts and wear them daily to

save my breath). Partaking in their worldview flashes me forward to a time, not so very long from now, where I probably won't be immersed in this kind of thinking, and won't have as many fresh bitch-slaps and observations to blog about. "I am tired of wishing I had the body I once had. It's been a long haul but I am learning to appreciate the one I possess now, in my 50s, with my great skin, health and intellect," wrote a woman named Lisa. At 42, I'm sick of it, too, but at the same time, a part of me obviously still wishes for mine to look closer to the ideal. I look forward to the time when my emotional life catches up with my intellectual one, and I can 100 percent fully revel in my other gifts, gifts that I already know will be my foundations going forward. I'm more than halfway there.

Their response reminds me that the Formerly years are just a film still in a (knock on wood) long life of moving images, and that someday, no doubt, I'll look back and think of how young I was when I wrote this book. And maybe how silly. And probably how good I looked. That's where I expect to be at some point, and time and the process of writing this book has moved me closer to feeling like the Formerly years are winding down.

When that happens, I will be Formerly a Formerly. Unlike a double negative, however, I'm pretty sure they don't cancel each other out, magically zapping me once again into my hot 20-something self. I don't know exactly what the phase beyond Formerly looks like, but I have a feeling I'll be keeping all the excellent developments from this period—

the groundedness, the confidence, the social ease and peace of mind—and hopefully putting some of the panic behind me. There will be new positive developments, and most likely, new things to panic about.

Right now, though, the Formerly shift feels very real to me, and worthy of the magnifying glass I've been applying to it. How I power through the Formerly years and the realizations I come to are critical to where I ultimately wind up. I don't think I'll be one of those women, who, like the one I corresponded with through my blog, is devoted to maintaining "hotness" until she dies, by any means necessary. I know I won't be a cougar, if they even really exist, feeding on youth like a vampire in hopes of extending my own youth. I definitely do not want to be one of those women you see everywhere in California, who look like a 25-year-old from behind, but from the front, between 45 and 60, tired, bleached-out and somehow both puffy and hollow at the same time. Their strange, misshapen facial features broadcast their unhappiness with themselves, and no matter what I wind up looking like, unhappiness is not an option.

What has made me happiest and most unhappy in my life, no matter how old I am, is the degree to which I feel free to express what I think, without fear of other people's reactions or their withdrawing their love. That fear is looking teeny tiny in the rearview mirror, which is to me the best thing about getting older. (I hope, of course, never to be the crazy old lady with blue hair and waaaay too much rouge on the bus who tells you you're a terrible parent and that you look trashy, to boot.) The other day, I had an episode that both made me feel as free as I've ever felt, and not a little old—and that was more than OK. It was transcendent.

I was rushing down 14th Street to go pick up my daughters, and this young woman with a clipboard angles over to me. She was wearing a light blue Greenpeace T-shirt, and was no more than 21. I shook my head no as I passed her, to indicate I didn't have time to stop.

"Oh, so you don't care about saving the planet. OK," she said.

I wanted to smack her—OK, yes, I am prone to violent fantasies when my blood sugar is too low, which it was then—but instead just rolled my eyes and kept walking. About 30 feet past where she was standing, however, I realized I couldn't contain my ire. I circled back.

"Excuse me, but you should know that what you said is really obnoxious. You don't know me, you don't know where I'm going, you don't know what groups I belong to or what my priorities are," I said (not for nothing, shifting my nylon shopping bag loaded with organic produce over to my other shoulder). "You're going to turn people off to your cause by saying things like that."

She protested that she asked me if I cared about saving the environment and I shook my head no, so she said, "OK, you don't care about saving the environment." She was simply innocently reflecting my own sentiments back at me. Right.

I said that I was saying no to stopping to chat with her, and she knew that full well. "I used to canvass for an environmental group"—I managed not to add, "when I was your age,"—"and I know how discouraging it can be, but you shouldn't assume you know why I'm not stopping. I'm going to pick up my children. I care about them, too." She tried to argue but I brushed her off and continued down the street, fuming.

I felt angry. I felt righteous. And then I felt like a crazy lady. OK, like a crazy OLD lady. Why did I even bother? She was a twit and I'd likely never see her again, and there I was explaining myself to her. I didn't like that she was a poor ambassador for Greenpeace, which does good work, but that wasn't really it. There was simply something about her smug, poreless, freckled face that made me want to give her what for, which I am aware is an old person's expression.

They say you really start to feel that you're getting older when your parents become creaky or infirm. I think it's when you begin to believe that you have something to teach snot-nosed NYU students with too much eyeliner who are exactly as likely to give a shit what you say as there is for the leaders of Palestine and Israel to hang out, smoke a bowl and come to a lovely, bi-lateral accord culminating in a giant group hug.

When I got to the Y to pick up my kids, I had a snack and felt better. Within minutes, I was drawn into looking at my daughters' drawings of fairies and ladybugs and finding their sweatshirts and listening to their tales of school yard dramas of hierarchy and exclusion. What to give them for dinner became my most pressing issue.

But I felt different than I had before my little contretemps with the canvasser. I felt true to myself—true to some larger truth—and not a little badass.

Indeed, I felt hot. No, not hot in the way I was when I was a big-haired man magnet in my 20s. And not hot like what Paris Hilton is alluding to when she gazes vapidly toward something and declares, "That's hot." (The words she'd be looking for if she thought to look are "exciting," "interesting," "current," "newsworthy.") But I felt hot, as in "on fire," "hot shit," and "not to be messed with." It was a different kind of hot, but the thermometer topped out just the same.

As hundreds of women have pointed out to me—when they hear the term "Formerly Hot" and think I mean that older women cannot be hot just because they don't look as they once did—hotness comes from within. I've always felt that way, even as my societally defined hotness has diminished. That Greenpeace incident reminded me that there are many measures of hotness, many ways of feeling hot, and that some are much easier to access as you get older. I, for one, am looking forward to finding out about the other ways, and seeing just how hot I can be.

ACKNOWLEDGMENTS

There simply isn't enough ink to thank all the amazing people who helped me channel my crazy into this book.

My husband, Paul Lipson, who did double and triple duty at home while I became one with my laptop; my girls, Sasha and Vivian, who point out my every Formerly flaw utterly without judgment and who, like most children, think getting older is thrilling; My amazing editor, Marnie Cochran, who finished my sentences in our first phone call, and my agent Rebecca Gradinger, who somehow makes me feel like her only client; my mom, Jessica Reiner, who began laughing at my jokes early and often; My dad, Anatole Dolgoff, who instilled in me the need to be heard; and Marge and Walter Lipson, for producing my husband, without whom I couldn't have produced this book (not to mention an armoire, a bureau, three night tables and a beautiful hand-crafted cutting board).

I really want to thank the FormerlyHot.com early adopters, including Robert Kempe, who made this book seem like a forgone conclusion as soon as the blog went up; and for making my website so fun and inviting, and then making it even more so; for her sage blog advice; Carol Hoenig, Kimberly Gagon and others for telling me their life stories, which indirectly helped me shape this book; and Julie Stark for her legal aid.

This book would not exist but for my very own "kept women," (and a few guys), my Formerly friends Andie Coller McAuliff, Kely Nascimento-DeLuca, Rhonda Davis, Julie Wright, Bárbara Herrnsdorf, Amy Redfield, Joel Jacobs, Ronni Siegel (the woman let me post a picture of her upper arms, for crying out loud!), Margaret Bravo, Hugh Siegel, Demetra Vrenzakis, Julie Bolt, Tula Karras, Alison Frank, Alan Blattberg, Emir Lewis, Marlene Merritt and (for letting me grill them about women's health), Melissa O'Neal, Rachel Fishman, Lauren Peden, Pam Redmond Satran and Alexandra Marshall, Harlene Katzman, Melissa Kantor, Judy Minor, Kristin Whiting, Carla Johnston Young, Marijke Briggs, Jenna McCarthy, Heather Greene, Freddi-Jo Bruschke, Rachel Berman, Marisa Cohen, Gina Duclayan, Karen Wolfe, Bennah Serfaty, Gina Osher, Jen Levine, Michele Barnwell, Susan Paley (for going all Hollywood on my ass), Michele Nader, Hanna Dershowitz and Maryn McKenna, Jennifer Maldonado and Heidi Schwartz.

Thanks, too, to Marika Guttman for being the (beautiful) face of the Formerly, Rachel Talbot for making my Formerly video, and for allowing her 29-year-old self to be whipped into a premature Formerly frenzy in marketing my book.

Hugs to the editors who encouraged me and my writ-